THE URDU DICTIONARY OF SHAAYARI

In English

3500 Must-know Urdu Words from the
Best Shers by Master Shaayars

Urdu Words in English and Hindi
Meanings in English

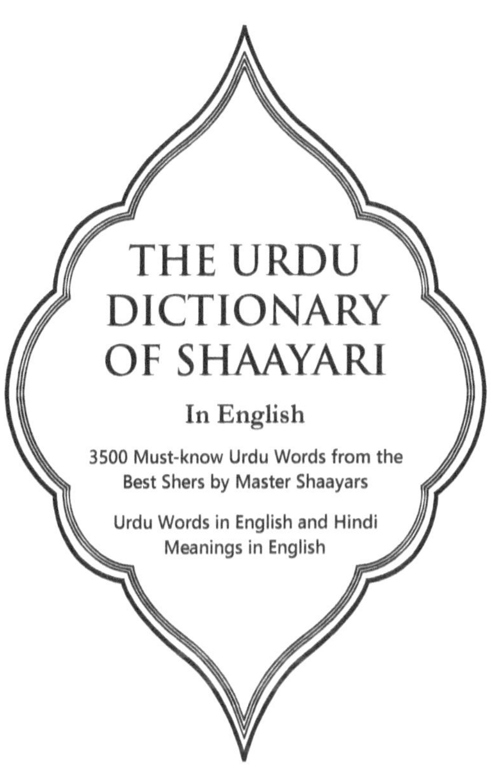

THE URDU DICTIONARY OF SHAAYARI

In English

3500 Must-know Urdu Words from the Best Shers by Master Shaayars

Urdu Words in English and Hindi Meanings in English

SUNIL GUPTA 'MUSTAQIL'

ZORBA BOOKS

ZORBA BOOKS

Published by Zorba Books, August 2023
Website: www.zorbabooks.com
Email: info@zorbabooks.com

Title: **The Urdu Dictionary of Shaayari**
Author Name: Sunil Gupta
Copyright © Sunil Gupta
Printbook ISBN :- 978-93-58967-70-8
Ebook ISBN :- 978-93-58967-71-5

The publisher under the guidance and direction of the author has published the contents in this book, and the publisher takes no responsibility for the contents, its accuracy, completeness, any inconsistencies, or the statements made. The contents of the book do not reflect the opinion of the publisher or the editor. The publisher and editor shall not be liable for any errors, omissions, or the reliability of the contents of the book.

Any perceived slight against any person/s, place or organization is purely unintentional.

Zorba Books Pvt. Ltd. (opc)
Sushant Arcade,
Next to Courtyard Marriot,
Sushant Lok 1, Gurgaon – 122009, India

To

Tulika

and

Tanmay

For opening new worlds to me

ACKNOWLEDGEMENT

I would like to acknowledge the deep debt I owe to Rekhta Foundation for opening the world of Urdu to me. Its world-class resources are heaven-sent for persons with negligible prior exposure to Urdu to become proficient in Urdu and partake of the joys and charms of Urdu. The Rekhta Dictionary is arguably the best online dictionary of Urdu and most of the meanings of the words (and compound-words) in this dictionary have been drawn from the Rekhta Dictionary.

PREFACE

Urdu Shaayari is the most popular genre of Urdu writing and is often the first exposure to the Urdu language for most of us, thanks to popular Hindi film songs and ghazals, which have enthralled generations in South Asia.

One can read Shaayari either in Urdu or in English or Hindi transliteration. Many of the Urdu words used in Shaayari are familiar to Indians for whom Urdu is not the first language but one still comes across unfamiliar words (or compound-words and phrases) the meaning of which are not known. And these unfamiliar words rob the entire sher of its magic! One may encounter an odd offline Urdu dictionary but the vast majority of words in such a dictionary are familiar and commonplace – almost none of the unfamiliar words found in well-known shers are found in these dictionaries.

Moreover, most offline dictionaries do not give the meanings of compound words or phrases. The correct nuance of these compound words is often different from the sense derived by merely putting together the meaning of individual words comprising the compound word.

Hence I have compiled 'The Urdu Dictionary of Shaayari – In English'. It is a comprehensive dictionary dedicated exclusively to Urdu Shaayari filled with 3500 Urdu words (and compound words or phrases) drawn from the most popular shers of the Masters of Urdu Shaayari of South Asia and the diaspora. The moment you encounter an unfamiliar word, just pop open 'The Urdu Dictionary of Shaayari – In English' and return quickly to the sher, which now resonates with meaning! The Urdu words are transliterated in English and arranged alphabetically for ease of reference, with the word meaning in English. In addition, the Urdu word is transliterated in Hindi since the pronunciation is rendered truer in Hindi.

Since this book is meant for those passionate about Urdu shaayari, I have avoided using grammatical terms which may be more relevant for serious students of the Urdu language.

Sunil Gupta 'Mustaqil'

A

Piine ko is jahaan main kaun sii mai nahiin magar
Ishq jo baanttaa hai vo aab-e-hayaat aur hai
Shamim Karhani

Samjhenge na agyaar ko agyaar kahaan tak
Kab tak vo mohabbat ko mohabbat na kahenge
Zaheer Dehlvi

Tumhaaraa husn aaraaish tumhaarii saadgii zevar
Tumhen koii zaruurat hii nahiin banne sanvarne kii
Asar Lakhnavi

Ham kisii aur vaqt ke hain asiir
Subh ke shaam ke rahe hii nahiin
Sarfraz Khalid

Aayaa na ek baar ayaadat ko tuu masiih
Sau baar main fareb se biimaar ho chukaa
Ameer Minai

Ziyaada kyaa tavaqqo ho gazal se
Miyaan bas aab-o-daana chal rahaa hai
Rahat Indori

Sabr par dil ko to aamaada kiyaa hai lekin
Hosh ud jaate hain ab bhii tirii aavaaz ke saath
Aasi Uldani

Tirchhii nazron se na dekho aashiq-e-dil-giir ko
Kaise tiir-andaaz ho siidhaa to kar lo tiir ko
Wazir Ali Saba Lakhnavi

Hamaaraa alamiya ye thaa ki ham-safar bhii hamen
Vahii mile jo bahut yaad aane vaale the
Waseem Barelvi

Tifl men buu aae kyaa maan baap ke atvaar kii
Duudh to dibbe kaa hai taaliim hai sarkaar kii
Akbar Allahabadi

A

Aab आब Water/Sheen/
Lustre/Sparkle/Edge of
sword

Aabaa आबा Ancestor/
Forefather

Aabaaii आबाई Ancestral

Aab-daar आब-दार
Brilliant/Polished

Aab-e-hayaat आब-ए-हयात
Elixir/Nectar/Water of
immortality

Aabgiin आबगीन Goblet/
Glass

Aab-juu आब-जू Stream/
Rivulet/Brook

Aab-e-ravaan आब-ए-रवां
Flowing water

Aab-o-daana आब-ओ-दाना
Water and food

Aab-o-giil आब–ओ–गील
Water and soil

Aab-o-taab आब-ओ-ताब
Splendour/Glory/
Brilliance

Aab-o-taaam-o-khvaab
आब-ओ-तआम-ओ-ख़्वाब
Water and food and
sleep

Aabruu आब्रू Respect/
Honour/Chastity/
Virginity/Status/Rank/
Fame/Credibility/
Brightness

Aadaab आदाब Greetings/
Salutations/Form of
address/Decorum/
Politeness/Civility/
Elegant manners

Aadam-e-khaakii आदम-ए-ख़ाकी Mortal man/ Adam made of clay/ Adam's dust

Aade aana आड़े आना Come in between

Aadil आदिल One who acts justly or equitably/ One whose testimony is trustworth

Aafaaq आफ़ाक़ Horizons/ The world

Aafaat आफ़ात Calamities

Aafat-talab आफ़त-तलब Calamity seeking

Aafiyat आफ़ियत Well-being/Security

Aafiyat-e-jaan आफ़ियत-ए-जान Well-being or protection or security of life

Aafriin आफ़रीन Well-begun/Applause/ Gratitude/Praise

Aafriinash आफ़रीनश Creation/Genesis

Aaftaab आफ़ताब Sun

Aagaahii आगाही Awareness/Cognizance/ Insight/Information/ Knowledge

Aagaz आगाज़ Beginning

Aahan आहन Iron

Aahang आहंग Sound/ Voice/Purpose/ Method/Rhythm/ Harmony/Tune/ Melody/Musical composition

Aah-o-zaarii आह-ओ-ज़ारी Lamentation/Wailing

Aah-o-zaariyaan आह-ओ-ज़ारियां Lamentation/ Hue and cry

Aahuu आहू Deer

Aaiin आईं Constitution/ Manifesto/Code/ Regulation/Statute/ Custom/Udage/ Method

Aaiina-daar आईना-दार Mirror-holder/Officer at Eastern court

Aaiinaa-daariyaan आईना-दारियां Act of reflecting

Aainda आइंदा Future

Aajizii आजिज़ी Humility/ Submissiveness/ Helplessness/ Inability/Meekness/ Powerlessness/Entreaty/ Supplication/ Hopelessness

Aakhirat आख़िरत Life after death/Hereafter

Aalaa-zarf आला-ज़र्फ़ Elegance (of manners)/ High capacity

Aalam आलम World/ Condition/Situation

Aalam-e-bashariyyat आलम-ए-बशरियत World of human beings

Aalam-e-iijaad आलम-ए-ईजाद World of innovation

Aalam-e-naa-paaedaar आलम-ए-ना-पाएदार Impermanent world

Aalam-e-taqriir आलम-ए-तक़रीर State of speech

Aalam-e-vajuud आलम-ए-वजूद World of existence

Aalim आलिम Doctor

Aaluud आलूद Tainted/ Soiled/Polluted

Aaluuda आलूदा Contaminated/Spoilt/ Polluted/Foul/Impure/ Unclean/Grimy/Sullied/ Soiled

Aaluuda-e-isyaan आलूदा-ए-इस्यां Polluted by sin

Aamaada आमादा Inclined/Predisposed/ Liable/Ready/Prepared/ Alert/Bent upon/ Tending towards

Aamaadgii आमादगी Inclination/Willingness/ Readiness/Preparedness

Aamaal आमाल Deeds/ Conduct/Behaviour

Aamaal-naama आमाल-नाम Balance sheet of deeds

Aamad आमद Arrival/
Visit/Advent/Income

Aamad-o-shud आमद-ओ-
शुद Coming and going/
Existence

Aamoz आमोज़ Learn/
Teaching

Aamozish आमेज़िश
Education/Teaching/
Learning

Aan आन Moment/
Dignity/Mode/Manner

Aaphii आपही You only

Aaraaii आराई
Embellishment/Origin/
Commencement/
Beginning

Aaraaish आराइश
Adornment

Aaraam-e-jaan आराम-
ए-जान Comfort of
life/Beloved/Children
(specially son)

Aarastaa आरस्ता
Decorated and
embellished

Aarif आरिफ़ Enlightened/
Wise/Knowing/Godly/
Pious/Mystic/Sufi/Sage

Aariyatii आरियति
Borrowed/Lent/
Transient

Aariz आरिज़ Cheek

Aarzii आरज़ी Accidental/
Temporary

Aasaab आसाब Nerves

Aasaaish आसाइश
Comfort/Luxury/
Prosperity/Happiness/
Facility/Ease/Amenity/
Repose

Aasaar आसार Indications/
Signs/Ruins/Relics

Aaseb आसेब Calamity/
Trouble/Madness/Evil
spirit/Demon/Illness/
Apparition/Ill-fortune/
Shock/Pain

Aaseb-zada आसेब-ज़दा
Haunted/Ghostly/
Under the influence of
an evil spirit

Aashiq-e-dil-giir आशिक़-
ए-दिल-रीर Sad lover

Aashkaaraa आशकारा Clear/Manifest/Visible/ Obvious

Aashob आशोब Crisis/ Calamity/Tumult

Aashob-e-maaash आशोब-ए-मआश Economic crisis

Aashob-e-navaa आशोब-ए-नवा Crisis of expression

Aashkaar आशकार Manifest/Visible

Aashnaa-e-hirs आशना-ए-हिर्स Knower of greed

Aashtii आश्ती Peace/ Accord/Concert/ Reconciliation

Aashufta आशुफ़्ता Distressed

Aashuftaa-mijaazon आशुफ़्ता-मिजाज़ों Those with distracted or perturbed moods

Aashufta-o-hairaan आशुफ़्ता-ओ-हैरां Distraction and amazement

Aashufta-saron आशुफ़्ता-सरों Afflicted people

Aasii आसी Sinner

Aasmaan आसमान Firmament/Sky

Aastaan आस्तां Abode of a holy man/Threshold/ Entrance/Door/ Entrance to a shrine

Aasuuda आसूदा Satisfied/ Content

Aatish आतिश Anger/ Rage/Passion/Fire/ Flame/Ignite

Aatish-e-namrood आतिश-ए-नमरूद Pyre made by Nimrod to burn Prophet Abraham

Aatish-fishaan आतिश-फ़िशां Dazzling/ Glowing/Volcano/Fire-spitting

Aatishiin आतिशीं Fire-like/Passionate/ Igneous/Ablaze/ Aflame/Fiery/ Glowing

Aavaaz-e-jamaal आवाज़-ए-जमाल Voice of beauty

Aayat आयत Verse of the Quran/Sign

Aazaada आज़ादा Liberated/ Free/Noble/Perfect/ Pure/Intact/Venerable

Aazmaaish आज़माइश Trial/Test/Experiment

Aazmaaish-e-qalb-o-nazar आज़माइश-ए-क़ल्ब-ओ-नज़र Trial of heart and perception

Aazurda आज़ुर्दा Distressed

Aazurdagii आज़ुर्दगी Woe/ Grief/Sorrow/Anger/ Depression/Displeasure/ Dejection/Distress

Abaa अबा Cloak/Gown

Abas अबस Futile/ Purposeless

Abjad अबजद Arrangement of 28 letters of the Arabic alphabet, each letter having a numerical value

Abru अबरू Eyebrow

Abru-e-araq-aluud अबरू-ए-अर्क़-अलूद Perspiring brow

Abtaar अबतार Dishevelled/Tousled

Abtarii अब्तरी Deteriorating/ Disorderly/Confusion/ Upset/Tired

Adaaegii अदाएगी Payment/Settlement

Adaa-fahm अदा-फ़हम One who appreciates grace and manners

Adl अदल Justice/Equity

Adam अदम Nonentity/ Lack/Want/Life after death/Void/Death

Adaavatein अदावतें Enmity

Adeeb अदीब Author

Adliya अदलिया Judiciary

Adnaa अदना Trivial/Petty/ Insignificant/Lowly/ Ignoble/Inferior/Small/ Mean/Little/Closer/ Near

Afkaar अफ़कार Thoughts/
Ideas/Opinions/
Theories/Worries/
Anxieties/Notions

Aflaak अफ़लाक Skies/
Heavens

Afshaan अफ़्शां Tinsel used
by women for make-up/
Scattering/Sprinkling/
Glittering golden powder

Afshaanii अफ़शानी
Dispersal/Scattering/
Strewing/Sparkling

Afsurda अफ़सुर्दा Sorry

Afsurdagii अफ़्सुर्दगी
Depression/Melancholy

Afsuun अफ़्सूं Enchantment

Afzuun अफ़ज़ूँ Much
greater/Much more

Agarche अगरचे Although/
Though/Even if/
Granted that

Agyaar अग्यार Strangers/
Opponents/Crafty/
Artful/Cunning/
Imposter

Ahad अहद One/Digit
one/Unique/God/
Having no partner (as an
attribute of Allah)

Aharman अहरमन God of
badness for Zoroastrians

Ahbaab अहबाब Friend/
Lover/Dear ones

Ahaadis अहादीस
Traditions or anectdotes
of companions of
Prophet Muhammad

Ahd अह्द Time/Season/
Epoch/Period/Reign/
Promise/Vow/Oath

Ahd-e-rafta अह्द-ए-रफ़्ता
Days gone by

Ahd-e-shauq अह्द-ए-शौक़
Age of love/Season of
love

Ahd-o-paimaan अह्द-
ओ -पैमान Treaty/
Agreement/Unique
promise/Vows and
promises/Pledge

Ahmak अहमक Idiot

Ahvaal अहवाल Condition/State/Affairs/Circumstances/Happenings/Events/Situation

Ahyaa अह्या Clans/Tribes/Families/The living

Aiina-daariyaan आईना-दारियाँ Acts of reflecting or holding mirrors

Ain ऐन Real/Exact

Ain-e-mastuuri ऐन-ए-मस्तूरी The very hiddenness

Ain-hijr ऐन-हिज्र Exactly like disunion/Separation itself

Ajal अजल Death

Ajdaad अजदाद Ancestors/Forefathers

Ajiizii अजीज़ी Helplessness/Humility/Submissiveness/Inability

Ajr अज्र Pay/Wage/Compensation/Reward for good deeds

Ajzaa अज्ज़ा Part/Portion/Section/Particles/Constituents/Ingredients/Element/Member

Akaarat अकारत Fruitless/Useless/Worthless/Gainless/Unavailing

Akhlaaq अख़लाक़ Virtue/Piety/Exemplary behaviour/Good manners/Ettiquette/Politeness/Ethics/Morals/Courtesy

Akhtar अख़्तर Star

Aks-e-muntashir अक्स-ए-मुन्तशिर Scattered reflection

Alaamat अलामत Sign/Token/Seal/Stamp/Indication/Symptom/Emblem/Insignia/Standard

Alaav अलाव Bonfire

Alal-elaan अलल ऐलान Public announcement

Alam अलम Pain/Grief/
Affliction/Anguish/
Torment/Flag/Prop/
Support

Alam-diin अलम-दीन Priest

Alamiya अलमिया
Tragedy/Tragic event

Alast अलस्त Wisdom

Aliim अलीम Learned/
Wise/Epithet for
God

Alqaab अलक़ाब Titles/
Honorific names/Form
of address in letter
writing

Amaa अमा Bowels

Amaan अमान Security/
Safety/Refuge

Amad-o-shud आमद-ओ-
शुद Comings and
goings

Aman-khvaah अमन-ख़्वाह
Seeker of peace

Ambaar अम्बार Heap/Pile/
Stack/Hoard/Stock/
Collection

Ambariin अम्बरीन Amber-
like/Of the colour
or odour like amber/
Fragrant

Amdan अमदन
Intentionally/Wilfully

Amla अमला Staff or
personnel/Material used
in a building/Bricks,
paint, etc

Amn अमन Security/Safety

Amrad अमरद Beardless/
Handsome tyouth

Amrad-parast अमरद-
परस्त Sodomite

Anaadil अनादिल
Nightingales

Anaasir अनासिर Elements

Anal-haq अनल-हक़ I am
God/Truth

Anal-bahar अनल-बहर I
am ocean

Andaaz-e-digar अंदाज़-ए-
दीगर In a different style

Andaliib अंदलीब
Nightingale

Andaruun अन्दरून Inner/Heart/Internal/The interior/Part of a house reserved for women

Andesha अंदेशा Apprehension/Anxiety/Fear/Doubt/Suspicion

Andoh अन्दोह Grief/Sorrow/Sorrowful/Full of grief/Torture

Andoh-rubaa अन्दोह-रुबा Eliminator of grief

Anfus अनफूस Spirituality

Angbiin अंगबीन Honey/Syrup

Angusht अंगुश्त Finger

Angusht-e-hinaaii अंगुश्त-ए-हिनाई Finger on which henna is applied

Aniis अनीस Companion

Anjum अंजुम Stars

Anjuman अंजुमन Society/Association

Anjuman-aaraaiyon अंजुमन-आराइयों Parties

Anqaa अंक़ा Very rare/Unavailable/Extinct/Mythical bird like phoenix/Woman with long neck

Anvaar अनवार Shining/Resplendent

Aqaarib अक़ारिब Kith and kin

Aqaliyat अक़लियत Minority

Aqd अक़्द Treaty/Contract/Agreement/Wedding/Marriage knot/Tie

Aqdas अक़दस Sacred

Aqiida अक़ीदा Tenet/Doctrine/Doctrine of faith or belief/Religion/Fundamental article of faith

Aqiidat अक़ीदत Attachment/Affection/Faith/Alliance

Aqdas अक़दस **Sacred**

Aqvaam अक़्वाम Nations/Peoples/Races

Aqvaam-e-aalam अक़्वाम-ए-आलम Nations of the world

Araaish अराइश
Adornment

Araq अरक़ Juice/Essence/
Sweat/Perspiration

Araq-aaluud अरक़-आलूद
Perspiring/Sweaty/
Covered with sweat

Araq-e-infiaal अरक़-
ए-इंफीआल Beads of
perspiration/Sweat of
repentance

Arbaab अरबाब Persons/
Masters/Lords/Possessors/
Supporters/Idols

Arbaab-e-hiram अरबाब-
ए-हिरम Possessors of
nobility or courage/
Those who are
courageous

Ariiza अरीज़ा Petition

Arkaan अरकान
Fundamentals/Parts

Arsa-e-hastii अरसा-ए-हस्ती
Life-time

Arsh अर्श Celestial/Heaven

Arsh-e-bariin अर्श-ए-बरीं
The highest heaven

Arzaan अरज़ां Of no value/
Cheap/Low priceed

Arzaanii अरज़ानी
Worthlessness/
Shoddiness/Cheapness/
Low price

Arz-o-samaa अर्ज़-ओ-समां
Earth and sky

Asaa असा Stick/Stave/
Support

Asaasa असासा Household
property/Wealth/
Belongings

Asbaab अस्बाब
Justifications/Motives/
Worldly goods/
Belongings

Ashad अशद Urgent/
Exigent

Ashk-baar अश्क-बार Tearful

Ashk-e-muztar अश्क-
ए-मुंतज़र Tears of
distressed or afflicted/
Forced by necessity

Ashk-e-nadaamat अश्क-
ए-नदामत Tears of
repentance

Aashuftagii आशुफ़्तगी
Distress/Affliction/
Perturbation/
Distraction/Anxiety/
Disorder

Asiir असीर
Prisoner

Asl अस्ल Pure/
Unadulterated/Real/
Legitimate/Pedigree/
Principal amount/
Actual incident/
Standard

Asr अस्र Late afternoon/
Time of the day before
sunset/Time/Age/
Epoch/Era

Asraar अस्रार Secrets/
Mysteries/Ghost/Evil
spirit/Spectre

Ataa अता Gift/
Concession

Atfaal अत्फाल Children/
Offspring

Atkheliyaan अठखेलियाँ
Mischief/Pranks

Atraaf अतराफ़ Sides/
Directions/Around/
Suburbs

Atvaar अतवार Habits/
Behaviour/Conduct/
Manners/Modes/Ways

Aubaashon औबाशों
Wanton/Wicked/
Licentious/Baddies

Auj औज Light

Auqaat औक़ात Status/
Time/Hours/Position/
Circumstances/Means/
Resources/Plural of time

Auraad औराद Sacred
chantings

Auraaq औराक़ Petals/
Pages

Ausaaf औसाफ़ Good
qualities

Avaamunnaas अवामुन्नास
Common public

Ayaadat अयादत Enquire
about patient's well-
being

Avval अव्वल First/
Foremost/First or early
part

Ayaan अयां Evident/Clear

Ayyaam अय्याम Times/ Duration/Seasons/ Menstrual period/Days

Ayyaam-e-shabaab अय्याम-ए-शबाब Time or days of youth

Ayyaar अय्यार Artful/ Cunning/Crafty/ Imposter

Ayyaarii अय्यारी Guile/ Cunningness/Slyness

Az अज़ From/Then/By

Azaa अज़ा Patience/ Endurance/ Condolence

Azaab अज़ाब Torment/ Curse/Agony/Anguish/ Divine punishment/ Troublesome affair/ Turbulent/Disorderly

Azaab-e-barq-e-baraan अज़ाब -ए-बर्क़-ए-बरां Calamity of lightning and rain

Azaab-e-daanish-e-haazir अज़ाब-ए-दानिश-ए-हाज़िर Curse of contemporary knowledge

Azaadaaron अज़ादारों Mourners

Azal अज़ल Eternity/ Beginning of time

Az-baam अज़-बाम Be revealed/Be exposed

Az-bas अज़-बस Vastly/ Very much/Extremely necessary

Az-bas-ki अज़-बस-कि That's why

Az-raah-e-sitam अज़-राह-ए-सितम By way of tyranny

Azhdahaa अज़्हदहा Python

Aziyyat अज़िय्यत Trouble/ Torment/Difficulty/ Torture/Annoyance/ Oppression

Aziizaan अज़ीज़ां Dear ones

Az-khud-rafta अज़-खुद-रफ्ता Automatically gone

Azm अज़्म Conviction/
Determination/
Fortitude/Intention/To
be or become great

Azmatein अज़मतें Majesties

Azm-e-junoon अज़्म-ए-जुनूं
Determination of frenzy

B

'Jauhar' tumhen nafrat hai bahut baada-kashii se
Barsaat men dekhenge ham inkaar tumhaaraa
Lala Madhav Ram Jauhar

Kuchh bataa tuu hii nasheman kaa pataa
Main to ai baad-e-sabaa bhuul gayaa
Majrooh Sultanpuri

Ham hain mushtaaq aur vo bezaar
Yaa ilaahii ye maajraa kyaa hai
Mirza Ghalib

Chupke se guzarte hain khabar bhii nahiin hotii
Din raat bhii kam-bakht javaanii kii tarah hain
Azlan Shah

Nayaa bismil huun main vaaqif nahiin rasm-e-shahaadat se
Bataa de tuu hii ai zaalim tadapne kii adaa kyaa hai
Chakbast Brij Narayan

Gosh paidaa kiye sunne ko tiraa zikr-e-jamaal
Dekhne ko tire, aankhon men basaarat dii hai
Haidar Ali Aatish

Mumkin nahiin ki bazm-e-tarab phir sajaa sakuun
Ab ye bhii hai bahut ki tumhen yaad aa sakuun
Jagan Nath Azad

Zamiin roii hamaare haal par aur aasmaan royaa
Hamaarii bekasii ko dekh kar saaraa jahaan royaa
Wahshat Raza Ali Kalkatvi

Jis jis se use rabt rahaa hai aur bhii log hazaaron hai.n
Ek tujhii ko be-mehrii kaa detaa kyuun ilzaam hai chaand
Ibn-e-Insha

Bint-e-havvaa huun main ye miraa jurm hai
Aur phir shaayarii to kadaa jurm hai
Sarwat Zehra

B

Baab-e-ilm बाब-ए-इल्म Chapter/Door of knowledge

Baab-e-iltijaa बाब-ए-इल्तिजा Door of requesting or pleading

Baadaa बादा Glass/Goblet

Baada-gulfaam बादा-गुलफ़ाम Rose-coloured wine

Baada-kashii बादा-कशी Drinking of wine

Baada-nosh बादा-नोश Wine drinker

Baadbaan बादबां Of or related to sails/Mast

Baad-e-fanaa बाद-ए-फ़ना After death

Baad-e-sabaa बाद-ए-सबा Morning breeze/Zephyr

Baadiya-paimaaii बादिया-पैमाई Wind measurement

Baag बाग Rein/Bridle/ The power to direct and control

Baahamii बाहमी Mutual

Baais बाईस Cause/ Occasion/Basis

Baalaaii-aamdanii बालाई-आमदनी Extra income

Baaliidgii बालीदगी Growth/Development/ Vegetation/Loftiness/ Maturity/Adolescence

Baam-e-haram बाम-ए-हरम Roof of Kaaba

Ba-andaaz ब-अंदाज़ By way of/According to

Ba-andaaza-e-khumaar ब-अंदाज-ए-ख़ुमार According to the intoxication

Baang-e-jaras बांग-ए-जरस Sound of caravan bells

Baanii-e-islaam बानी-ए-इस्लाम Founder of Islam

Baar बार Load/Burden

Baaraan बाराँ Rains

Baare बारे About/In connection with/At last

Baar-e-khaatir बार-ए-ख़ातिर Unpleasant/Disagreeable

Baar-e-nashaat बार-ए-नशात Burden/onus of ecstasy/

Baargaah बारगाह Audience hall/Court/Presence/Palace/Mansion/Holy or royal or august or noble presence

Baar-haa बार-हा Many times

Baar-var बार-वर Endure/To bear fruit

Baatil बातिल False/Untrue/Wrong/Incorrect/Spurious/Unreal/Fictitious/Unsound/Null/Void/Ineffectual/Annulled/Abolished

Baatin बातिन Internal/Mind/Heart/Inner self/Among Allah's names/Inside/Hidden self

Baavar बावर Confidence/Faith/Trust/Belief/Credible/Trustworthy/Net for trapping rabbits, deer, etc

Baaz बआज़ Few/Some/Sundry/Diverse

Baaz बाज़ Refrain/Desist

Baazgasht बाज़गश्त Echo/Return/Restitution/Restoration/Reaction/Return of voice/Reversion/Relapse

Baaziicha बाज़ीचा Playground/Toy/Child's play/Fun/Play/Frolic/Sport

Baaz-pasiin बाज़-पसीन
Last/Hindmost

Ba-dam ब-दम At the
moment

Ba-dastuur ब-दस्तूर As
before/As usual/In
status quo/Customarily

Bad-gumaan बद-गुमां
Disloyal/Distrustful/
Suspicious

Bad-havaasii बद-हवासी
Insensitive/Harassed

Bad-mazaa बद-मज़ाBad
taste

Badr बद्र Full moon/
Accounting mistake

Bad-zan बद-ज़न
Mistrustful/Suspicious

Ba-gard ब-गर्द Around

Baguulaa बगूला
Whirlwind/Windstorm

Ba-haazir ब-हाज़िर
Apparently

Ba-hangaam-e-sahar
ब-हंगाम-ए-सेहर Time of
morning

Ba-haq ब-हक़ True

Bahar बहर Without

Bahar-haal बहर-हाल At
any rate/In any case

Bahar-taur बहर-तौर
Anyway

Baham बहम Along with/
Together

Bahara बहराProfit/
Success/Fortune/
Prosperity/Blessing

Bahara-yaab बहरा-याब
One who gets profit/
Usurer/Profiteer/
Partner/Gainer/
Blessed/Happy/
Prosperous/ Fortunate/
Lucky/Successful

Bahisht बहिश्त Heaven

Bahr बह For/Ocean/In
any/By every/To every
(way,mean,etc)

Bahr-e-khudaa बह-ए-ख़ुदा
For God's sake

Bahr-e-taksiin बह
-ए-तक्सीन For
satisfaction sake

Bahr-e-tavahhum बह्-ए-तवहहुम Ocean of superstition or delusion or imagination

Bahr-o-bar बह्-ओ-बर Ocean and land/The Globe/The World

Baht बह्त Pure/ Unadulterated/ Unmixed/Only

Baiat बइअत Swearing allegiance/Homage/ Fealty

Ba-ibrat ब-इबरत To learn from example

Baiid बईद Beyond

Bain बैन Distance/Interval/ Lamentation/Wailing for the dead

Bairuun बैरूँ Outside

Baitullah बैतुल्लाह House of God/Kaaba at Mecca

Bajaa बजा Suitable/ Appropriate/Right/ Correct

Ba-jaae बजाए In place of/ Instead of/In lieu of

Ba-juz ब-जुज़ Except/ Beside

Bakhiilii बख़ीली Avarice/Parsimony/ Niggardliness

Bakhiya-gar बखिया-गर Tailor

Bakhiya-garii बखिया-गरी Stitching

Bakht बख़्त Destiny/Luck

Bakht-e-khufta बख़्त-ए-ख़ुफ़्ता Hidden destiny

Bakul-e-be-samar बकुल-ए-बे-समर Tree without fruit

Band-a-qabaa बंद-ए-क़बा Belt or knot of tunic

Banjaara-mizaajii बंजारा-मिज़ाजी Metaphorically vagabond

Bansa-navaaz बंसा -नवाज़ Lord/God/Sir/Patron/ One who takes care of someone

Bapaa बपा In progress/ Going on/Afoot

Baqaa बक़ा Perpetuity/ Permanence/Eternity/ Immortality/Survival/ Continuance/Security/ Safety

Ba-qadr ब-क़द्र Appreciate/ To the extent of/ Amounting to/By or on the quantity of/By the power (of)/By means (of)

Ba-qadr-e-zauq-e-tamannaa ब-क़द्र-ए-ज़ौक़-ए-तमन्ना To the extent of good taste or value of desire

Ba-qaul ब-क़ौल According to the saying (of)

Bar बर At/Bear fruit/Land

Barahnagii बरहनगी Nudity

Bar-aks बर-अक्स On the contrary/As against/In opposition(to)

Barg बर्ग Leaf

Bargashta बर्गशता Angry/ Upset/Turned back/ Changed

Barg-e-gul बर्ग-ए-गुल Leaf of flower/Rose petal

Barham बरहम Angry/ Vexed/Inflamed

Barhamii बरहमी Confusion/ Anarchy/Anger/ Vexation/Displeasure/ Trouble/Wrath/ Convulsion/Wrath

Barhana बरहना Naked

Barhana-paa बरहना-पा Bare feet

Bar-khud-galat बर-ख़ुद-ग़लत Self-mistake

Barpaa बरपा Happen

Barq-paaron बर्क़-पारों Shards/pieces of lightning

Barsar बर्सर On/In

Bar-sar-e-paikar बर-सर-ए-पैकर Engaged in fight/Fighting/Pitted against/Self-sustained/ Accomplished

Bartarii बरतरी Excellence/
Eminence/Superiority/
Ascendancy/Altitude

Bar-waqt बर-वक़्त
Opportune

Basaarat बसारत Vision

Bashaarat बशारत Good
news/Glad tidings/
Revelation

Bashar बशर Man/Human
being

Bashariiyat बशरीयत
Human beings

Basiirat बसीरत Sight/
Insight/Foresight/
Prudence/Knowledge/
Understanding/
Intelligence/
Discernment/Vision

Baski बस्कि Although

Bast-e-zulf बस्त-ए-जुल्फ़
Hair tied

Basyaar बसयार Many/
Much/Multitudinous

Ba-tadbiir ब-तदबीर By
strategy

Ba-tang ब-तंग Distressed/
Vexed/In dire straits

Ba-vaqt ब-वक़्त At the time

Bayaabaan बयाबाँ
Wilderness/Desert

Bayaabaanon बयाबानों
Wilderness (p)

Bayaaz बयाज़ book in
which poet writes verse/
Account book

Ba-zaahir ब-ज़ाहिर
Apparently/Outwardly/
Ostensibly/Externally/
In appearance

Bazm-e-suruur बज़्म-ए-
सुरूर Party of ecstasy

Bazm-e-tarab बज़्म-ए-तरब
Gathering of happiness

Be-aah-e-sahar-gaahii
बे-आह-ए-सहर-गाही
Sightless awakening

Be-ahaadiis बे-अहादीस
Without traditions
or anecdotes of
companions of Prophet
Mohammad

Be-amaan बे-अमान
Without refuge

Be-asaas बे-असास Without heritage

Be-baak बे-बाक़ Fearless

Be-bahra बे-बहरा Deprived of benefit/Unlucky/ Poor

Bedaad बे-दाद Injustice/ Tyranny/Oppression/ Violence/Iniquity

Bedaar बेदार Awakened

Be-gaana बे-गाना Strange/ Unconcerned/Not related/Estranged/ Foreign/Alien/Exotic

Begaana-var बेगाना-वर
Like a stranger or alien/ Apathetic/Without enthusiasm

Be-haiat बे-हैअत
Amorphous/Unshaped/ Shapeless/Formless/ Unformed

Be-his बे-हिस Insensitive

Be-hisii बे-हिसी Without feeling

Be-huzuur बे-हुज़ूर Absent/ Not present/Non- existent/Disgraceful

Bejaa बेजा Improper/ Misplaced/Unlawful/ Beyond limit/Wrongly/ Improperly

Be-kaifii बे-कैफ़ी Dull/ Drab/Insipid/ Uninteresting

Bekalii बे-कली Restlessness

Be-kanaar बे-कनार
Boundless/Without a shore/Infinite

Be-karaan बे-करां
Limitless/Boundless/ Immense/Unbounded/ Shoreless

Be-kas बे-कस Helpless

Bekasii बेक़सी
Helplessness/ Friendlessness/Destitute

Be-khatar बे-ख़तर Free from danger/Fearlessly/ Safe

Be-khirad बे-ख़िरद
Irrational

Be-manzaarii बे-मंजारी
Without any scenery

Be-mehrii बे-मेहरी Loveless

Be-muravvat बे-मुरव्वत
Unkind/Uncivil/
Inhuman

Be-naqat बे-नकत Without
using diacritical dots

Be-navaa बे-नवा Destitute/
Indigent

Be-naziir बे-नज़ीर
Matchless/Unique/
Peerless

Be-niyaazaanaa बे-
नियाज़ाना Careless

Be-niyaaz बे-नियाज़
Carefree/Independent/
Without want

Be-niyaazi बे-नियाज़ी
Aloofness/Air of
carelessness/Without
want/Carefree

Be-paayaan बे-पायां
Immeasurable

Be-panaah बे-पनाह
Without shelter

Be-parha बे-परहा Deprived
of benefit

Be-par-o-baalii बे-पर-
ओ-बाली State of being
without wings and
hair/Helplessness/
Compulsion

Be-qasd बे-क़स्द Unintended

Be-rabt बे-रब्त Disjointed/
Disconnected/Unrelated/
Irrelevant/Unconnected

Be-rabtiyon बे-
रब्तियों (Plural)
Unconnectedness/Lack
of synchronisation

Be-ridaaii बे-रिदाई Without
a shawl/scarf/covering

Be-rutba बे-रुत्बा Without
rank or status

Be-saakhta बे-साख़्ता
Spontaneously/
Extempore/Natural/
Of it own accord/
Extemporaneously/
Undisguised/Unartificial

Be-saakhta-pan बे-साख़्ता-
पन Spontaneity

Be-saarbaan बे-सारबान Without camel driver

Be-sabaat बे-सबात Mortal/Transitory

Be-sar-o-saamaaniyon बे-सर-ओ-सामानियों Homeless

Be-sar-o-saamaanii बे-सर-ओ-सामानी Without bag and baggage

Beshtar बेश्तर For the most part/Mostly/Generally/Often

Be-suruur बे-सुरूर Without ecstasy

Be-suud बे-सूद Useless

Betaabaana Restless/Hurriedly/Impatiently

Be-zaar बे-ज़ार Bored

Be-zaarii बे-ज़ारी Boredom/Unhappiness/Displeasure/Disgust/Annoying

Be-zarii बे-ज़री Poverty

Bhaan-bhod भान-भोड़ Tear and mangle

Bharam भरम Reputation/Trust/Secret/Repute/Good character/Deceit/Doubt/Suspicion

Bhulaapa भुलापा Forgetting

Biim बीम Despair

Biinaaii बीनाई Eyesight/Vision

Biinash बीनाश Vision

Bila बिला Without

Binaa बिना Basis

Bint बिन्त Daughter

Bint-e-havvaa बिन्त-ए-हव्वा Daughter of Eve

Bint-ul-inab बिन्त-उल-इनब Daughter of grape/wine

Birog बिरोग Separation from beloved

Bisaat बिसात Capacity/Power/Bedding/Carpet/Chess-board

Bismil बिस्मिल Slaughtered animal/Afflicted lover

Bojhal बोझल Heavy/ Burdened/Loaded/ Weighty/Laden

Boriya बोरिया Coarse rug/ Sack/Mat made of palm trees

Bosiida बोसीदा Rotten/ Decayed/Worn- out/Old/Ancient/ Dilapidated

Bos-o-kanaar बोस-ओ- कनार Kissing and fondling/Dalliance/To do love

Bul-havas बुल-हवस Very greedy

But-e-pindaar बुत-ए-पिंडार Idol of self-respect or dignity

Buud बूद Existence/Being/ Happened/Was

Buud-o-baash बूद-ओ- बाश Whereabouts/ Way of life/Manner of living/Subsistence/ (Metaphorically) Abode/ Residence/Existence

Buu-qalamoon बू- क़लमून Variegated/ Diversity

C

Koii chaaraa nahiin duaa ke sivaa
Koii suntaa nahiin khudaa ke sivaa
Hafeez Jalandhari

Hogii na chaaraagar tirii tadbiir kaargar
Ham ko khud apne zakhmon kii chaahat hai aaj-kal
Ameer Nehtauri

Aao to mere sahn men ho jaae raushnii
Muddat guzar gaii hai charaagaan kiye hue
Ashhad Bilal Ibn-E-Chaman

Dil vo kaafir hai ki mujh ko na diyaa chiin kabhii
Bevafaa tuu bhii use le ke pashemaan hogaa
Bekhud Dehlvi

Na chitvan aap kii thahrii na dil miraa thahraa
Use sukuun ho to is ko bhii kuchh qaraar rahe
Ashique Akbarabadi

Bade saliiqe se duniyaa ne mere dil ko diye
Vo ghaao jin men thaa sachchaaiyon kaa charkaa bhii
Majeed Amjad

Tum chashm-e-haqiiqat se agar aap ko dekho
Aaiina-e-haq men dil-e-insaan hai maujuud
Bahadur Shah Zafar

Ruuthne aur manaane kii haden milne lagiin
Chashm-poshii ke saliiqe the shikaayaat ke saath
Parveen Shakir

Shaayad tire labon kii chatak se ho jii bahaal
Ai dost muskuraa ki tabiiat udaas hai
Abdul Hamid Adam

Aaina dekh ke khurshiid pe karte hain nazar
Phir chhupaa lete hain vo chehra-e-anvar apnaa
Bekhud Dehlvi

C

***Chaao-chuuz* चाओ-चूज़** Dalliance/Fondness/ Gratifying every wish/ Caressing

***Chaara* चारा** Remedy/ Option/Way

***Chaaraagar* चारागर** Doctor

***Chaar-girah* चार-गिरह** Four knors/Span

***Chakiidan* चकीदन** Throw

***Champaii* चम्पई** Light yellow colour

***Chang* चंग** A kind of harp or lute

***Charaagaan* चारागां** Display of lights/ Illumination/ Illuminating of lamps

***Charaag-kade* चराग़-कदे** Niches or places for lamps

***Charkaa* चर्का** Tear/Gash/ Scratch/Hack

***Charkh* चर्ख** Sky/Celestial orb/Potter's wheel/ Carousel/Hyaena/ Fortune/Destiny

***Chashma-e-aab-e-hayaat* चश्म-ए-आब-ए-हयात** Fountain of immortality

***Chashma-e-haivaan* चश्मा-ए-हैवान** Spring or fountain of immortality

***Chashm-e-haqeeqat* चश्म-ए-हक़ीक़त** Eye of reality

***Chashm-e-tan-aasaan* चश्म-ए-तन-आसान** Eye of indolent or lazy

***Chashm-poshon* चश्म-पोशों** Those who turn the eyes away/Affecting not to see or hear/Conniving to overlook/Palliating/Excusing

***Chatak* चटक** Bloom/Break open/Briskness

***Chehra-e-anvar* चेहरा-ए-अनवर** Bright face

***Chiin* चीन** Wrinkle/Frown

***Chiin-e-peshaanii* चीन-ए-पेशानी** Wrinkles on the forehead

***Chitvan* चितवन** Appearance/Look/Glance/The state of seeing someone with love and affection

***Chob* चोब** Wood/Stick

D

Tum jo chaaho to mire dard kaa darmaan ho jaae
Varna mushkil hai ki mushkil mirii aasaan ho jaae
Bedam Shah Warsi

Dasht jaisii ujaad hain ankhen
In dariichon se khvaab kyaa jhaanken
Siraj Faisal Khan

Ham ajnabii hain aaj bhii apne dayaar men
Har shakhs puuchhtaa hai yahii tum yahaan kahaan
Waheeda Naseem

Uthe jaate hain diida-var sabhii aahista aahista
Ye duniyaa motabar logon se khaalii hotii jaatii hai
Ateeq Asar

Vo hii aasaan karegaa mirii dushvaarii ko
Jis ne dushvaar kiyaa hai mirii aasaanii ko
Parveen Umm-E-Mushtaq

Bas ek lamha tire vasl kaa mayassar ho
Aur us visaal ke lamhe ko daaimii kiyaa jaae
Hammad Niyazi

Tukde hue the daaman-e-hastii ke jis qadar
Dalq-e-gadaa-e-ishq ke paivand ho gae
Saba Akbarabadi

Dalaael se khudaa tak aql-e-insaanii nahiin jaatii
Vo ik aisii haqiiqat hai jo pahchaanii nahiin jaatii
Makhmoor Dehlvi

Gae bhii jaan se aur koii mutmain na huaa
Ki phir difaa na karne kii ham pe tohmat thii
Shariq Kaifi

Manzil-e-ibrat hai duniyaa ahl-e-duniyaa shaad hain
Aisii dil-jamii se hotii hai pareshaanii mujhe
Chakbast Brij Narayan

D

Daad दाद Praise/Applause

Daag-e-alam दाग-ए-अलम Spot of tragedy

Daaim दाइम Perpetual/ Eternal/Continuing always/Lasting/ Perpetually/ Continuously/ Permanent

Daaimii दाइमी Permanent

Daakhil-e-rasm-o-rivaaz दाख़िल-ए-रस्म-ओ-रिवाज़ Part of tradition and custom

Daalaan दालान Vestibule/ Covered way/Corridor/ Yard/Lobby/Open hall/ Courtyard

Daam दाम Snare/Bait/ Trap/Chain/Price/Cost

Daamaan दामान Foot of hill/Skirt/Part of garment below chest/ Refuge/Protection/ Peace

Daamaan-e-falak दामान-ए-फ़लक Expanse of sky

Daaman-e-hasti दामन-ए-हस्ती Expanse of life

Daam-e-shunidaan दाम-ए-शुनिडां Net of listening

Daaman-giir दामन-गीर Attached (to)/Adherent/ Dependant/Claimant/ Accuser/Plaintiff/ Seeking redress(from)

Daaman-kashaan दामन-कशान Ignoring

Daaman-e-maadar दामन-ए-मादर **Lap** of mother

Daam-e-ajal दाम-ए-अजल
Clutches of death

Daaman-kashaan दामन-कशां Walking with dignity and grace/ Dragging or trailing the skirt/Turning away (from)/Abandoning/ Shunning

Daanaa दाना Sage/Wise man/Wise/Learned/ Wise/Prudent

Daanaaii दानाई Wisdom

Daang दांग Direction

Daanista दानिस्ता Knowingly/Wittingly/ Deliberately

Daar दार Gallows

Daar-e-faanii दार-ए-फ़ानी House of mortality

Daar-o-rasan दार-ओ-रसन Stake and rope/Gallows

Daavar दावर Judge

Daavar-e-mahashar दावर-ए- महशर Judge on judgement day

Dabiiz दबीज़ Coarse/Thick

Dabistaan दबिस्तां School/ School of thought

Dafatan दफ़अतन Suddenly

Dafiina दफ़ीना Hidden treasure

Daftar दफ़्तर Office/Large volume/Book/Archive/ Record-office

Daftar-e-amal दफ़्तर-ए-अमल Record of good and bad

Dahan दहन Mouth

Dahqaan दहक़ां Farmer/ Peasant

Dahr दहर World/Era/ Time/Period

Dakhal दख़ल Occupancy/ Occupation/Possession

Dakhiil दख़ील Intruder/ Invader/Admitted/ Allowed entrance/ Friend/Accomplice/ Guest/Familiar/ Intimate/Introduced

Dalaael दलाएल Arguments

Dalak दलक Trembling/ Shaking/Tottering/ Quaking/Vibration/ Shock/Blow

Daliil-e-kaamraani दलील-ए-कामरानी Evidence of success

Dalq दल्क़ Patched garment

Dalq-e-gadaa दल्क़-ए-गादा Parched garment of dervishes of love

Dam दम Moment

Damaadam दमादम Repetitive/Rhythmic/ Continuously/Frantically leaping & making noise in a fit of esctasy

Dam-ba-dam दम-ब-दम Continuously/ Constantly/Incessantly/ In every moment/ Repeatedly

Dam-e-naza दम-ए-नज़ा Time of death/ Near death/Being in the agonies of death/ Moment preceding death

Dam-e-tahriir दम-ए-तहरीर Time of writing

Danish दानिश Knowledge/ Learning/Wisdom

Danish-e-hazir दानिश-ए-हाज़िर Contemporary knowledge

Daraa दरा Caravan bells

Daraaz दराज़ Long/High/ Exalted/Tall/Lengthy/ Extended/Crack/Split/ Break

Darakhshaan दरख़्शां Shining/Brilliant/ Resplendent

Darakht दरख़्त Tree

Dar-badarii दर-बदरी Vagrancy

Dardmand दर्दमंद Sympathiser/ Friend

Dar-guzar दर-गुज़र Overlook/Pass by/Turn aside (from)/Neglect

Dar-haqeeqat दर-हक़ीक़त Matter of fact/In fact

Dariida दरीदा Torn/Rent/ Ragged/Tired/Upset

Dariya-e-hairat दरिया-ए-हैरत River of wonder

Dariya-nosh दरिया-नोश Excessive drinker

Darke दरके Damaged

Darmaan दरमान Medicine/Remedy/ Cure/Solution

Dar-parda दर-पर्दा Concealed/Veiled/ Hidden/Secret/Privately

Darpesh दरपेश Under consideration/Placed before

Dars दर्स Lesson/Lecture/ Course of studies/ Advice

Dars-e-ishq दर्स-ए-इश्क़ Lesson of love

Dars-e-yaar दर्स-ए-यार Lesson related to beloved

Dar-guzar दर-गुज़र Excuse/Forgive/Turn aside (from)/Neglect/ To pass by or over/ Overlook

Daruud दरुद Praise of Prophet Mohammad

Daruun दरूं Inside

Daryaaft दरयाफ़्त Discovery

Dashnaa दशना Dagger

Dasht दश्त Forest

Dasht-e-imkaan दश्त-ए-इमकान Forest of possibility

Dasht-e-laa-makaan दश्त-ए- ला-मकान Infinite desert

Dasht-navardii दश्त-नवर्दी Wandering in the desert

Dastaar दस्तार Turban

Dastaras दस्तरस Reach/ Access/Within one's power/Ability/Power

Dastar-khvaan दस्तर- ख्वां Piece of cloth spread on the ground on which food is served

Dast-ba-dast दस्त-ब-दस्त
Hand to hand/Quickly/
Hand to had (fight)/
Back to back/Face to
face

Dast-basta दस्त-बस्ता
Humbly/Respectfully/
With folded hands

Dast-e-aduu दस्त-ए-अद्‌
Enemy's hand

Dast-e-chup दस्त-ए-चुप
Left hand

Dast-e-daadaar दस्त-
ए-दादर Hand of the
creator

Dast-e-ras दस्त-ए-रस Right
hand

Dastiyaab दस्तियाब
Available/Procurable/
Attained

Dast-nigar दस्त-निगार
Needy/In need of

Daulat-e-sar दौलत-ए-सर
Wealth of the mind

Daulat-e-faqr-o-fanaa
दौलत-ए-फ़क्र-ओ-फ़ना
Wealth of asceticism

Daur-e-daamaan दौर-ए-
दामां Time or period of
peace or protection of
refuge

Daur-e-jahaan दौर-ए-जहां
Times of the world

Dayaar दयार Territory/
Region

Dhaaras धारस Consolation

Dhab ढब Habit/Position/
Style/Method/Habit/
Way/Conduct

Dhanak धनक
Rainbow

Dhare धारे Current/Stream

Dhaulaa धौला White/
Clear/Bright/Any white
thing/White colour

Difaa दिफ़ा Defence

Digar दिगर Other

Diida-e-hairaan दीदा-ए-
हैरां Discerning eyes

Diida-e-khuun-baar दीदा-
ए- ख़ून-बार Weeping
with or due to extreme
pain

Diidanii दीदनी Worth seeing/Fit to be seen/Observable/Visible

Diida-var दीदा-वर Sharp-sighted/Perspicacious/Visionary/Perceptive/Connoisseur/One who appreciates and enjoys

Diigar दीग़ार Other/Another/Once more/Again

Diivaar-e-tarab दीवार-ए-तरब Wall of joy, delight, happiness

Dil-afgaar दिल-अफ़्गार Heart-broken/Degected/Melancholy/

Dil-e-aagaah दिल-ए-आगाह Prudent/Vigilant

Dil-e-haziin दिल-ए-हज़ीं Sad heart

Dil-e-naa-kardaa-kaar दिल-ए-ना-करदा-कार Heart whose efforts are futile

Dil-e-naashaad दिल-ए-नाशाद Disappointing heart

Dil-fareb दिल-फ़रेब Heart-alluring/Enticing/Charming

Dil-giir दिल-गीर Sad/Melancholy

Dil-jamii दिल-जमी Encouragement

Dil-juu दिल-जू Searcher of heart/One who gives solace or encourages

Dil-navaaz दिल-नवाज़ Kind/Benevolent

Dil-pazir दिल-पज़ीर Acceptable to the mind and soul/Pleasing/Pleasant/Delightful

Dil-shikan दिल-शिकन Heart-breaking

Dil-zada दिल-ज़दा Wounded or stricken to the heart/Wounded

Diraa दिरा Insight/Bell/Caravan bell

Divaana-var दीवाना-वर With frenzy

Divaar-e-tarab दीवार-ए-तरब Wall of delight or joy or happiness

Do-aalam दो-आलम Universe/Both worlds

Doshiiza दोशीज़ा Virgin/Beautiful girl

Doshiizgii दोशीज़गी Virginity/Maidenhood

Dui दुइ Two/Both/Dualism/Polytheism

Durd-e-tah-e-jaam दुर्द-ए-तह-ए-जाम Dregs or sediment at the bottom of a glass of wine

Dur-e-nayaab दुर-ए-नायाब Rare pearl

Dushman-e-arbaab-e-vafaa दुश्मन-ए-अर्बाब-ए-वफ़ा Enemy of those who are faithful or constant

Dushvaarii दुश्वारी Difficulty

Duud दूद Smoke/Haze/Mist/Vapour

Duur-as-tariiq दूर-ए-तरीक़ Atheist/Iniquity

Duzdeeda दुज़दीदा A furtive glance/By stealth/Clandestinely/Sly/Stolen/Purloined/Pilfered/

Duzd-e-hinaa दुज़्द-ए-हिना White spaces left in the hand after application of henna

E

Chal to saktaa thaa main bhii paanii par
Main ne dariyaa kaa ehtiraam kiyaa
Anjum Saleemi

Safar pe nikle hain ham puure ehtimaam ke saath
Ham apne ghar se kafan saath le ke aae hain
Iqbal Azeem

Rishton kaa etibaar vafaaon kaa intizaar
Ham bhii charaag le ke havaaon men aae hain
Nida Fazli

Mohabbaten to faqat intihaaen maangtii hain
Mohabbaton men bhalaa etidaal kyaa karnaa
Hasan Abbas Raza

Main jurm kaa etiraaf kar ke
Kuchh aur hai jo chhupaa gayaa huun
Jaun Eliya

Diye bujhe to havaa ko kiyaa gayaa badnaam
Qusuur ham ne kiyaa ehtisaab us kaa thaa
Wazir Agha

Le ke dil rakh lo kaam aaegaa
Go abhii tum ko ehtiyaaj nahiin
Dagh Dehlvi

Mujhe tumhaarii nigaahon pe etimaad nahiin
Mire qariib na aao badaa andheraa hai
Saghar Siddiqui

Ab har ik shakhs hai eazaaz talab
Shahr men chand makaan the pahle
Azhar Inayati

Nahiin ki mujh ko qayaamat kaa e'tiqaad nahiin
Shab-e-firaaq se roz-e-jazaa ziyaad nahiin
Mirza Ghalib

E

Eajaaz एअजाज़ Miracle

Eazaaz एअज़ाज़ Honour/
Respect

Ehtaraam एहतराम Respect

Ehtimaam एहतिमाम
Preparation/Planning/
Care

Ehtiraaz एहतिराज़ To
avoid/Guarding against/
Abstaining from/Being
cautious of/ Abstinence/
Avoidance

Ehtisaab एहतिसाब
Accountability/
Reckoning/Estimating/
Computing/Accounting
for/Casting or making
up accounts

Ehtiyaaj एहतियाज
Necessity/Need/Want

Ehtiyaaz एहतियाज़
Retribution/Reward/
Exchange/Alternative of
anything

Etibaar ऐतिबार Trust/
Belief/Respect/Regard/
Credence/Faith/
Credibiity/Esteem

Etibaaraat एतिबारात
Reliance/Trusts

Etidaal ऐतिदाल Moderation

Etimaad एतिमाद
Confidence/Faith/
Trust/Reliance/
Dependence

Etiqaad ऐतिक़ाद
Conviction/Religious
belief

Etiraaf ऐतिराफ़ Admission/
Confession/Agree

F

Jo rang-e-ishq se faarig ho us ko dil nahiin kahte
Jo maujon se na takraae use saahil nahiin kahte
Wasif Dehlvi

Ab kar ke faraamosh to naashaad karoge
Par ham jo na honge to bahut yaad karoge
Meer Taqi Meer

Ham ishq men hain fard to tum husn men yaktaa
Ham saa bhii nahiin ek jo tum saa nahiin koii
Lala Madhav Ram Jauhar

Kyuun na firdaus men dozakh ko milaa len yaarab
Sair ke vaaste thodii sii jagah aur sahii
Mirza Ghalib

Khamoshii dil ko hai furqat men din raat
Ghadii rahtii hai ye aathon pahar band
Lala Madhav Ram Jauhar

Sunaa hai us kii siyah-chashmagii qayaamat hai
So us ko surma-farosh aah bhar ke dekhte hain
Ahmad Faraz

Har ek jism ruuh ke azaab se nidhaal hai
Har ek aankh shabnamii har ek dil figaar hai
Shahryar

Fitna-gar shokhii-e-hayaa kab tak
Dekhnaa aur na dekhnaa kab tak
Zaheer Dehlvi

Tumhaare qaum ke bachchon men hai taaliim kaa fuqdaan
Ye gutthii sakht pechiida hai is ko jald suljhaao
Ahmaq Phaphoondvi

Kaam the ishq men bahut par 'miir'
Ham hii faarig hue shitaabii se
Meer Taqi Meer

F

Faakhta फ़ाख्ता Dove

Faanii फ़ानी Mortal/ Perishable/Transitory

Faanuus फ़ानूस Chandelier

Faaqa फ़ाक़ा Fasting/ Starvation/Poverty/ Penury

Faaqa-kashii फ़ाक़ा-क़शी Starvation

Faaqa-masti फ़ाक़ा-मस्ती Cheerfulness in adversity

Faaqon फ़ाकों Poverty/ Want/Fast

Faarig फ़ारिग Free/ Unoccupied/ Disengaged/Discharged

Faatah-e-aalam फ़तह-ए-आलम Conqueror of world

Faatiha फ़ातिहा Opening chapter of Quran/ Commencement/First part (of a thing)/Prayers for the dead

Fahm फ़हम Understanding/ Comprehension/One who understands/ Intelligence

Fahmi फ़हमी Understanding

Fahrist फ़हरिस्त List

Faiz फ़ैज़ Success/Grace/ Favour

Faizaan फ़ैज़ान Grace/ Beneficence/Good influence

Faiz-e-husn फैज़-ए-हुस्न Rewards or gifts of beauty

Faiz-yaab फैज़-याब Benefitted/Blessed in life

Falak-bos फ़लक़-बोस Kissing the sky

Falak-e-duun फ़लक़-ए-दूं Ill-fate/Lower sky

Falak-e-siflaa फ़लक़-ए-सिफ़ला Ignoble or sordid fortune

Fanaa फ़ना Death

Faqiih फ़क़ीह Theologian

Faqr फ़क़्र Poverty

Faraag फ़राग़ Leisure/Repose/Freedom/To be free (from)/Disengagement/To cease(from)

Faraagat फ़राग़त Cessation from labour/Time for rest/Comfort/Interval/Ease/Relaxation

Faraaham फ़राहम Amassed/Gathered/Collected/Accumulated/Available/Obtained

Faraakh फ़राख़ Ample/Spacious

Faraakhi फ़राख़ी Generosity

Faraakhi-e-aflaak फराख़ी-ए-अफ़लाक Generosity of the skies

Faraamosh फ़रामोश Forgetful

Faraasiis फ़रासीस Of or belonging to France/French

Faraavaan फ़रावां Abundant/Ample/Plenty/Copious/Excess

Faraaz फ़राज़ Height/Elevation/High/Elevated

Farang फ़रंग European

Fard फ़र्द Unique/Single/Unmatched/List/Catalogue

Fardaa फ़र्दा Tomorrow

Fareb-khurdaa फ़रेब-खुर्दा One who has been deceived

Farhang फ़रहंग Dictionary/Vocabulary/Wisdom/Intellect/Elegance/Refinement

Farhat फ़रहत Pleasure/Happy/Cheerful/Joy/Pleasuring

Farmaan-ravaa फ़रमान-रवा Ruler/Sovereign/One entitled to rule

Farog फ़रोग़ Splendour

Farosh फ़रोश Seller

Faroshi फ़रोशी Selling (used in composite i.e. mewa-faroshi that is selling of mewa)

Farsang फ़रसंग League (3.75 miles)

Farsuuda फ़रसूदा Weathered/Eroded/Spoilt by time or age/Effaced/Outmoded/Worn-out

Fashaar फ़शार Defuse

Fasiil फ़सील Boundary/City wall

Fasl-e-gul फ़स्ल-ए-गुल Springtime/Season of spring

Fasurda फ़सुर्दा Disappointed/Old/Sad/Worn-out

Fataah-e-aalam फ़ताह-ए-आलम Conqueror of the world

Faut फ़ौत Death/Passing away/Expire/Escaping/Being lost

Fazaa फ़ज़ा Ambience

Faziilat फ़ज़ीलत Excellence

Figaar फ़िगार Afflited/Fatigued/Wounded

Fikr-e-jamiil फ़िक्र-ए-जमील Beautiful ideas or thoughts

Fil-haqeeqat फ़िल-हक़ीक़त Indeed

Finjaan फिंजां Cup for drinking qahwa

Firdaus फ़िर्दौस Paradise/Garden

Firdaus-e-gum-gashta फ़िरदौस-ए-गुम-गश्ता
Lost paradise

Firqa फ़िर्क़ा Sect/
Community/Religious
sect or cult/Group of
persons with similar
belief

Firqa-bandii फ़िर्क़ा-बंदी
Organisation of people
into sects/castes/
polarization

Fishaan फ़िशां Spreading/
Diffusing/Scattering/
Strewing/Throwing

Fishaar फ़िशार Pressing or
squeezing/Pressure

Fitna फ़िला Temptation/
Mutiny/Revolt/
Discord/Conflict/
Anarchy/Mischief/
Crime/One who
creates mischief/Craze/
Beloved/Seduction/
Evil/Sin/Madness/
Sweetheart

Fitna-gar फ़ितना-गर
One who provoked/
Mischievous

Fitraak फ़ित्राक Saddle
straps/Cords fixed to a
saddle for hanging game
from

Fitrat फ़ितरत Inherent
quality/Nature/
Disposition/Wisdom/
Faith

Fiza फ़िज़ा Space/Air
space/Atmosphere

Fugaan फ़ुगां Cry of
distress/Lamentation/
Wail/Clamour/Crying

Fuqaraa फ़ुक़रा Beggar/
Mystic/Sufi

Fuqdaan फ़ुक़दान
Shortage/Dearth

Fuqdaan-e-uruuj-rasan-o-daar फ़ुक़दान-ए-उरूज-
रसन-ओ-दार Dearth of
exaltation of rope and
scaffold

Furqat फ़ुर्क़त Separation
(of lovers)/Absence (of
friend or beloved)

Fusuun फुसूँ Enchantment/ Sorcery/Magic/Spell/ Incantation

Fuzuun फुज़ून Many/ Plenty/Increasing

G

Sair kar duniyaa kii gaafil zindagaanii phir kahaan
Zindagii gar kuchh rahii to ye javaanii phir kahaan
Khwaja Meer Dard

Raat din gardish men hain saat aasmaan
Ho rahegaa kuchh na kuchh ghabraaen kyaa
Mirza Ghalib

Ham dard ke maare hii giraan-jaan hain vagarna
Jiinaa tirii furqat men kuchh aasaan to nahiin hai
Azeem Murtaza

Rahii na taaqat-e-guftaar aur agar ho bhii
To kis umiid pe kahiye ki aarzuu kyaa hai
Mirza Ghalib

Phuul barse kahiin shabnam kahiin gauhar barse
Aur is dil kii taraf barse to patthar barse
Bashir Badr

Hai gaib-e-gaib jis ko samajhte hain ham shuhuud
Hain khvaab men hunuuz jo jaage hain khvaab men
Mirza Ghalib

Main jii rahaa huun gam-kada-e-rozgaar men
Terii mohabbaton kaa sahaaraa liye hue
Shakeel Badayuni

Baith jaataa huun jahaan chhaanv ghanii hotii hai
Haae kyaa chiiz gariib-ul-vatanii hotii hai
Hafeez Jaunpuri

Itnii girhen lagii hain is dil par
Koii khole to kholtaa rah jaae
Tahzeeb Hafi

Guzishta saal ke zakhmo hare-bhare rahnaa
Juluus ab ke baras bhii yahiin se niklegaa
Rahat Indori

G

Gaaebaana ग़ायबाना Absence/Secretly/ Invisibly

Gaafil ग़ाफ़िल Inattentive/ Neglectful/Unmindful/ Sound asleep/ Unconscious/Oblivious (to)

Gaah गाह Sometimes

Gaalib ग़ालिब Superior/ Higher/Victorious/ Predominant/ Conquerer/Often/In plenty/The most/

Gaalibaan ग़ालिबां Most probably/Apparently/ For the main part/ Mostly/Chiefly/ Principally/Upon the whole

Gaam गाम Footstep/Step/ Pace (of horse)

Gaamii गामी Steps/Pace/ Foot/Accompanying/ Companion

Gaaza ग़ाज़ा Reddish cosmetic powder for brightening the skin/ Rouge/Blusher/Face powder/

Gab-gab ग़ब-ग़ब Double chin

Gabr गब्र Infidel/Pagan/ Fire-worshipper/ Zorastrian

Gadaa गदा Beggar/ Mendicant

Gadaagar गदागर Beggar/ Mendicant

Gadaagarii गदागरी
Beggary

Gadaaii ग़दाई Begging/
Beggary/Poverty/Mean/
Misery/Wretched/
Insignificant

Gadaa-navaaz गदा-नवाज़
Rewarding beggar

Gadlaa ग़दला Dirty/
Turbid/Muddy/Foul/
Soiled/Heavy

Gah गह House

Gahe गाहे Often/
Sometimes/Occasionally

Gahnaae गहनाए Eclipsed

Gaib ग़ैब That which is
hidden/mysterious/
unseen/Divine

Gaib-e-gaib ग़ैब-ए-ग़ैब
Mystery of mysteries

Gairat ग़ैरत Self-respect/
Honour/Shame/
Modesty/Dignity/Sense
of honour/Jealousy

Galiiz ग़लीज़ Dirty/Filthy/
Faeces/Stool

Gam-gusaar ग़म-गुसार
Comforter/Consoler

Gam-kadaa ग़म-क़दा
Abode of sorrow/
mourning

Gam-khvaar ग़म-ख़्वार
Sympathiser/Consoler/
Comforter/Sympathiser

Gam-khvaarii ग़म-
ख़्वारी Condolence/
Consolation

Gamnaak ग़मनाक Tragic

Gamza ग़म्ज़ा Coquetry/
Amorous Glance/
Wink

Gam-kadaa ग़म-कदा
Abode of sorrow

Gam-zada ग़म-ज़दा
Afflicted/Aggrieved

Gandum गंदुम
Wheat

Ganiimat ग़नीमत
Blessing/Boon/
PrizePlundr/Booty/
Littlein quantity or
number but
sufficient

Ganjiina गन्जीना Repository/Treasury/ Wealth/Granary/ Compilation/Store/ Magazine

Garaaben गराबें Curved part of the edge of a sword or axe/Crows or ravens

Garaan गरां Unpleasant/ Dear/Costly

Garaz ग़ारज़ Intention/ Object/Purpose/End

Garche गर्चे Although/ Even/If

Gardan-zadanii गर्दन- ज़दनी Deserve to be beheaded

Gard-e-mahtaab गर्द- ए-महताब Dust of or movement or revolution around the moon

Gard-e-malaal गर्द-ए- मलाल Cloud of regret

Gardish ग़ार्दिश Revolution/ Change of fortune/ Vicissitudes

Gardish-e-ayyaam ग़ार्दिश -ए-अय्यां Vicissitudes of fortune

Gardish-e-prakaar ग़ार्दिश –ए- प्रक़ार Motion of compass

Garduun गर्दूं Sky/ Heavens/Firmament

Gariibaan-e-chaman गरीबां-ए-चमन Exiled from one's country

Gariib-ul-vatan ग़ारीब- उल-वतन Foreigner

Gariib-ul-vatanii ग़ारीब- उल-वतनीExile

Garm ग़ार्म Passionate

Garm-e-tavaaf गर्म- ए-तवाफ़ Eager to circumambulate

Garq ग़ार्क़ Drowned/ Obsessed

Garq-e-dariyaa-e-muhiit ग़ार्क़-ए-दरिया-ए-मुहीत Drowned in encircled river

Garqaab ग़ार्क़ाब Drowned

Garqaabii ग़र्क़ाबी Drowning

Gash ग़श Fainting/Stupor

Gazal-saraa ग़ज़ल-सरा One who reads or recites gazals

Gazal-saraaii ग़ज़ल-सराई Reading or reciting or singing Gazal

Gaziida ग़ज़ीदा Injured

Ghaag घाघ Wily/Sly/ Seasoned/Veteran/ Experienced

Gaarat ग़ारत Destruction/ Pillage/Plunder/Ravage

Gaarat-gar-e-diin ग़ारत-गर-ए-दीन Destroyer of religion

Gesuu-e-taabdaar गेसू-ए-ताबदार Lustrous tresses

Ghafoor ग़फ़ूर Merciful

Gham-e-farda ग़म-ए-फ़र्दा Tomorrow's sorrow

Gham-e-gitii ग़म-ए-गिती Sorrow of life

Ghurbat ग़ुरबत Poverty/ Misery/Woe/ Uncommonness/State of being an alien or foreigner or traveller/In an alien land

Ghutii घुटी To be depressed/To be spent/ Diminished

Giibat ग़ीबत Speaking ill of someone behind his back

Gil गिल Soil

Gila-e-barhana-paaii गिला-ए-बरहना-पाई Complaint of being barefoot

Gilaurii गिलौरी Paan/Betel leaf

Giraan गिरां Weight/ Burden/Grief/ Unpleasant/Expensive

Giraanbaarii गिरांबारी Hardship

Giraanii गिरानी Heavier/ Weighty/Dearness/ Expensive

Giraan-maaya गिरां -माया Exquisite/Precious

Girafta-dil गिरफ़्ता-दिल
Sad/Arrested by heart

Girah गिरह Knot/Joint/
Tie

Gird गिर्द About/Near/
Around/In the
environs/Behind/
Round/Circumference

Girdaab गिर्दाब Vortex/
Whirlpool

Girhein गिरहें Knots

Girya गिर्या Weeping/
Lamentation/Crying/
Tears

Giryaan गिरयां Wailing/
Crying

Giryaan-naak गिरयां-नाक़
Weeping/In tears

Gor गोर Tomb

Gor-e-gariibaan गोर-ए-
गरीबां Burial ground for
poor or strangers

Gosh गोश Ear

Goshe गोशे Corners

Goyaa ग़ोया As if

Gubaar-e-dil गुबार-ए-

दिल Trouble of mind/
Vexation/Displeasure/
Affliction/Harboured
bitterness/Resentment

Gudaaz गुदाज़ Molten/
Dissolved/Melted/Soft and
plump/Tender/Gentle/

Gud-dhaanii गुड़-धनी
Sweet made from
molasses and rice crisps

Gufta-e-Ghalib गुफ़्ता-ए-
ग़ालिब Said by Ghalib

Guftaar गुफ़्तार Speaking/
Telling/Speech/
Conversation

Gauhar गौहर Gem/Pearl/
Sharpness of sword/
Descent/Origin

Gul-afshaanii गुल-
अफ़शानी Showering of
flowers/Eloquence

Gul-andaam गुल-अंदाम
Flower-limbed/Slender/
Delicate

Gul-chiin गुलचीं Florist/
Flower gatherer or
plucker/Gardener

Gul-e-tar गुल-ए-तर Fresh flower/Beloved with beautiful face

Gulfaam गुलफ़ाम Red/Rosy/Delicate/Beautiful

Gul-fishaan गुल-फ़िशां Strewn with flowers

Gul-gasht-e-chaman गुल-गश्त-ए-चमन Walk in the garden

Gulguun गुलगूं Rose-coloured/Red-coloured

Gul-karii गुल-कारी Flower painting/Tapestry

Guluu गुलू Throat

Gulzaar-e-hast-e-buud गुलज़ार-ए-हस्त-ए-बूद Garden of what is and what was

Gumaan गुमां Surmise/Conjecture

Gum-gashta गुम-गश्ता Lost/Missing

Guncha-dahan गुंचा-दहन Bud-faced

Guncha-lab गुंचा-लब Bud of lips/One with a mouth like a bud

Gunjaaish गुंजाइश Scope

Gunjaan गुंजान Dense/Compact/Thick/To sing a song

Gurbat गुर्बत Poverty/Misery/Uncommonness

Gurez गुरेज़ Escape/Evasion/Avoid/Run away/Aversion/Dislike/Abhorrence/Flight/Turning to the real subject after a prelude

Gurezaan गुरेज़ां Fleeing/Run away from/Escape from

Guruub गुरूब Setting (of sun/moon)/Sunset

Gusl गुस्ल Complete purificatory washing of the whole person/Bathing/Ablutions

Gustaakhii गुस्ताख़ी
Arrogance/
Presumptousness/
Rudeness/Insolence

Guun गूँ Merit

Guzar-auqaat गुज़र-
औक़ात Livelihood/
Sustinence

Guzishta गुज़िश्ता
Previous

H

Ilaaj kii nahiin haajat dil-o-jigar ke liye
Bas ik nazar tirii kaafii hai umr-bhar ke liye
Munawwr Badayuni

Abhii chhutii nahiin jannat kii dhuul paanv se
Hanuuz farsh-e-zamiin par nayaa nayaa huun main
Iftikhar Mughal

Hadaf bhii mujh ko banaanaa hai aur mere hariif
Mujhii se tiir mujhii se kamaan maangte hain
Manzoor Hashmi

Ik umr sunaaen to hikaayat na ho puurii
Do roz men ham par jo yahaan biit gaii hai
Habib Jalib

Ab in huduud men laayaa hai intizaar mujhe
Vo aa bhii jaaen to aae na etibaar mujhe
Khumar Barabankavi

Agar vo aaj raat hadd-e-iltifaat tod de
Kabhii phir us se pyaar kaa khayaal bhii na aaegaa
Yaqoob Yawar

Hadiis-e-shauq kahen yaa karen hayaat kii baat
Har ek baat tirii chashm-e-iltifaat kii baat
Faiz Tabassum Tonsvi

'Gaalib' vo shakhs thaa hama-daan jis ke faiz se
Ham se hazaar hech-madaan naamvar hue
Hargopal Tufta

Aurat ke khudaa do hain haqiiqii o majaazii
Par us ke liye koii bhii achchhaa nahiin hotaa
Zehra Nigaah

Betaab hai kamaal hamaaraa dil-e-haziin
Mehmaan saraa-e-jism kaa hogaa ravaana kyaa
Haidar Ali Aatish

H

Haa-e-duur-daraaz हा-ए-दूर-दराज़ Far-reaching

Haail हाईल Impediment/ Obstacle/Preventing/ Hindering/Intervening/ Restraining/Disturbing

Haajat हाजत Necessity/ Need/Requirement

Haakim हाक़िम Ruler/ Judge/Master/Chief

Haamil हामिल Carrier/ Bearer/Porter/Coolie/ Having any quality or property

Haasil हासिल Gain/ Result/Profit/Outcome/ Revenue/Result

Haasil-e-duniya हासिल-ए-दुनिया Gain or benefit or advantage of the world

Haasil-e-kun हासिल-ए-कुन Achieved

Habaab हबाब Bubble

Hadaf हदफ़ Target

Hadd-e-iltifaat हद्द-ए-इल्तिफ़ात Limit of kindness

Hadd-e-nazar हद्द-ए-नज़र Line of sight/FHorizon/ As far as the eye can see

Hadiis-e-shauq हदीस-ए-शौक़ Story of love or desire or passion

Hadiya हादिया Gift/ Present/Conclusion ceremony of Quran where parent gives teacher a gift

Hafiz हाफ़िज़ Keeper/ Guardian/Protector/ One who memorizes the Quran

Hafiza हाफ़िज़ा Good memory

Haif हैफ़ Alas/Ah/Pity

Haihaat हायेहात Alas/Woe to me/Begone

Haivaan हैवान Eternity

Hamal हमल Pregnancy

Hajv हज्व Lampoon/ Satire/Reproach

Hajv-e-mai हज्व-ए-मये Seeming praise but lampooning wine

Hakiiqat-e-muntazar हक़ीक़त-ए-मुंतज़र Awaiting reality/The hereafter

Halaak हलाक़ Destruction

Halaavat हलावट Sweetness/ Deliciousness/Comfort/ Relief/Relish taste

Halal हलल Legitimate/ right

Halq हल्क़ Wind pipe/ Gullet/Throat

Halqa हल्क़ा Links (of a chain)/Fraternity

Halqa-e-daam-e-khayaal हल्क़ा-ए-दाम-ए-ख़याल Links of the chain of thought

Halqa-e-naa-moatbar हल्क़ा-ए-ना-मोतबरCircle of unreliable

Halqa-e-yaaraan हल्क़ा-ए-यारां Circle of friends

Ham-aahangii हम-आहंगी Agreement/Harmony/ Concord

Hama-daan हमा-दान All-knowing/Omniscient

Ham-asron हम-अस्रों Contemporaries

Hama-tan हमा-तन Wholly/Entirely

Hama-tan-chashm हमा-तन-चश्म All eyes

Hama-tan-gosh हमा-तन-गोश All ears

Ham-damon हम-दमों Sympathisers/Friends/Companions

Ham-kanaar हम-कनार Embracing

Ham-kalaam हम-कलाम Conversing together

Ham-navaa हम-नवा Singing in unison/Friend/Companion

Ham-raaz हम-राज़ Confidant/Secret holder

Ham-safiir हम-सफ़ीर Companion/Friend/Fellow-songster

Ham-safiiron हम-सफ़ीरों Fellow-songsters or whistlers

Ham-sajnon हम-सजनों Of the same lovers

Hamvaar हम-वार Even/Level/Smooth/Consistent/Equable/Seamless

Ham-zaad हम-ज़ाद Alter ego

Hangaama-e-hastii हंगामा-ए-हस्ती Chaos of life

Hangaama-ha-e-shauq हंगामा-ह-ए-शौक़ Chaos of love

Hanuuz हनूज़ Yet

Haq हक़ Truth/Right/Favour/Due/Claim

Haq-biin हक़-बीं Truth-seeker

Haqaaeq हक़ाइक़ Facts/Realities

Haqiiqat-e-muntazar हक़ीक़त-ए-मुंतज़र Awaited reality or truth

Haqiiqii हक़ीक़ी Essential/Certain/Bona fide/True/Real/Actual/Just/Accurate/Own

Haqiir हक़ीर Despicable/Contemptible/Vile/Mean/Insignificant/Abject/Base/Least

Haq-go हक़-गो One who speaks for justice

Haq-goii हक़-गोई Telling truth

Haraarat हरारत Fever/Heat/Warmth/Ardour/Zeal/Passion/Frenzy

Harakat हरकत Act/Action/Mischief/Misdemeanour

Haram-e-paak हरम-ए-पाक Holy mosque

Harbaa हर्बा Arms/Weapons

Har-chand हर-चंद However/Although/How-so-ever

Harf हर्फ़ Word

Harf-e-mukarrar हर्फ़-ए-मुक़र्रर Repeated word

Hariif हरीफ़ Rival/Opponent/Competitor/Peer/Mate/Audacious/Impudent/Clever/Cunning

Hariim हरीम House/Part of the house reserved for women/Sanctuary/Walls of Kaaba/Sared place

Hariis हरीस Greedy/Covetous/Avaricious/Greedy or covetous person

Har-suu हर-सू In all directions

Hasb-e-aarzuu हज़्ब-ए-आरज़ू According to wish

Has-e-rozgaar हस-ए-रोज़गार Mundane life

Hashmat हश्मत Dignity/Pomp/Parade/Riches/Wealth

Hashr हश्र Tumult/Commotion/Lamentation/Wailing/Gathering/Congregation/Doomsday/Day of judgement

Hasratein हसरतें Unfulfilled desires/Regret/Grief/Intense sorrow

Hast-o-buud हस्त-ओ-बूद What is and what was/ All that is or was/The present and past

Havaadis हवादिस Disasters

Havaala हवाला Reference

Havaale हवाले Custody/ Care/Possession

Havaas हवास Senses

Hayaat हयात Life/ Existence/Soul/Spirit

Hayaat-aaraaii हयात-आराई Embellishment of life

Hayaat-o-mamaat हयात-ओ-ममात Life and death

Hayaatii हयाती Life/ Existence/Of a lifetime

Hazb-e-aarzuu हज़्ब-ए-आरज़ू According to wish

Haziin हज़ीं Melancholy/ Sad/Sorrowful

Hech-madaan हेच-मदाँ Ignorant

Hiddat हिद्दत Severity or degree of heat

Hiila-e-taksiin हीला-ए-तक्सीन Artful contrivance or device or excuse/Pretense of satisfaction

Hiile हीले Excuses

Hijaaz हिजज़ Holy land for Islam/western province of S rabia which includes Mecca and Medina/ Barrier or obstacle/Rope

Hijje हिज्जे Spelling/ Division of words into phonetic syllables

Hijrat हिजरत Migration

Hikaayat हिकायत Story/ Tale/Narrative

Hikmat हिकमत Knowledge/Science/ Wisdom/Cleverness

Hilaal हिलाल Crescent/ New Moon

Himmat-e-aalii हिम्मत-ए-आली High level of courage

Himaayat हिमायत
Support/Protection/
Defence

Hiqaarat हिक़ारत
Contempt/Scorn/
Disdain/Disgrace/
Affront

Hiraas हिरास
Disappointment

Hiraasaan हिरासां
Disappointed

Hiram हिरम Noble/
Exalted brother

Hirmaan हिरमां
Despondence/
Disappointment/
Misfortune/Denial (of a
thing, to a person)

Hisaar हिसार Enclosure/
Fence/Fortification/
Rampart/Fort/
Castle

Hissar-bandii हिसार-बंदी
To fortify

Hissar-e-zaat हिसार-ए-ज़ात
Boundary of self

Hosh-rubaa होश-रुबा

One who steals reason/
Beloved

Huduud हुद्दूद Limits/
Boundaries

Hukkaam हुक्क़ाम
Governers/Rulers/
Commanders/
Authorities/Officers/
Judges/Magistrates

Hungaam हंगाम A suitable
moment/Period of time

Huruuf हुरूफ़
Words

Husuul हुसूल Acquisition/
Attainment/Getting/
Profit/Advantage

Husn-e-aakhir हुस्न-ए-
आख़िर Ultimate beauty

Husn-e-amal हुस्न-ए-अमल
Elegance of action/
deliverance

Husn-e-bayaan हुस्न-ए-बयां
Elegant description

Husn-e-be-sabaat हुस्न-
ए-बे-सबात Mortal or
transitory beauty

***Husn-e-jahaan-e-soz* हुस्न-ए-जहां-ए-सोज़** Beauty which singes the world

***Husn-e-maliih* हुस्न-ए-मलीह** Wheatish beauty

***Husn-parastii* हुस्न-परस्ती** Worship of beauty

***Huu* हू** Dread/Fear/Terror/Desolation

***Huuk* हूक़** Howl/Cry of pain/Shooting pain/Extreme sorrow causing a deep sigh

***Huvaidaa* हुवैदा** Manifest/Clear/Evident/Open

***Huzuur* हुज़ूर** Presence

I

Chaman tum se ibaarat hai bahaaren tum se zinda hain
Tumhaare saamne phuulon se murjhaayaa nahiin jaataa
Makhmoor Dehlvi

Muddat se iltifaat mire haal par nahiin
Kuchh to kajii hai dil men ki siidhii nazar nahiin
Imdad Ali Bahr

Tum takalluf ko bhii ikhlaas samajhte ho 'faraaz'
Dost hotaa nahiin har haath milaane vaalaa
Ahmad Faraz

Laakhon men intikhaab ke qaabil banaa diyaa
Jis dil ko tum ne dekh liyaa dil banaa diyaa
Jigar Moradabadi

Har ik ko nahiin hotaa irfaan mohabbat kaa
Har ik ko mohabbat kii jaagiir nahiin miltii
Anjana Sandhir

Bas ek sang-e-dar se rahaa rishta umr-bhar
Aisaa nahiin milegaa ibaadat-guzaar dil
Amritanshu Sharma

Barat rahaa huun main lafzon ko ikhtisaar ke saath
Ziyaada likhnaa hai aur diary bahut kam hai
Shakeel Azmi

Main yuun udaas huun imshab ki jaise rang-e-gulaab
Khizaan kii chaap se be-saakhta utar jaae
Aitbar Sajid

Shab aaj kii vo mire naam karne vaalaa hai
Ye inkishaaf huaa thaa ki raat biit gaii
Taimur Hasan

Koii bhii shakl mukammal kitaab ban na sakii
Har ek chehra yahaan iqtibaas jaisaa hai
Muztar Haidri

I

Ibaadat इबादत Prayer

Ibaadat-guzaar इबादत-गुज़ार Devout/One who offers prayers

Ibaarat इबारत Composition/Mode of expression/Passage of a book/Sentence/Word/Phrase/Style of writing

Ibhaam इबहाम Ambiguity

Ibrat इब्रत To take lesson or admonition/Warning/Admonition/An example

Ibrat-saraa-e-dahr इब्रत-सरा-ए-डहर World as an admonitory inn of warning

Idgaah इदगाह Amalgamation

Idraak इद्राक़ Senses

Iflaas इफ़लास Poverty

Ifshaa इफ़शा Disclosure

Iftaar इफ़्तार Breaking a fast/A slight repast with which a fast is broken

Iifaa ईफ़ा Fulfilment/Observance/Performance/Satisfaction

Iijaad ईजाद Invention/Contrivance

Iimaanii ईमानी Conviction and belief/Related to belief/Believer

Ilm-e-nihaanii इल्म-ए-निहानी Knowledge of the occult or hidden secrets

Iisaar ईसार Sacrifice/
Selflessness

Iltifaat इल्तिफ़ात
Considerations/
Cogitation/
Contemplation/
Reflection/Scrutiny/
Examination

Iltimaas इल्तिमास Request

Iizaa ईज़ा Pain/Harm

Ijaabat इजाबत
Acceptance/Answering
or acceptance of prayer/
Compliance/Consent

Ijaara इजारा Monopoly/
Lease/Letting land on
lease/Letting a house/
Contract

Ijz इज्ज़ Helplessness/
Powerlessness/
Humility/Modesty

Ik-guuna इक-गूना
Continuous

Ikhlaas इख़्लास Sincerity/
Great affection

Ikhraaj इख़राज To remove
or secretive

Ikhtilaaf इख़्तिलाफ़
Dissension/
Disagreement/
Discord/Contradiction/
Difference/Opposition/
Changes/ Revolution

Ikhtilaafaat इख़्तिलाफ़ात
Differences

Ikhtilaat इख़्तिलात Union/
Confluence

Ikhtisaar इख़तिसार
Brevity/Synopsis/
Abbreviation/Summary/
Precis/Abridgement

Ikhtitaam इख़्तिताम
End/Completion/
Termination/Finish/
Close/Accomplishment

Ikhtiyar इख़्तियार Authority

Ikraam इकराम Honour/
Respect

Iksiir इक्सीर Cure-all
medicine/Panacea/
Elixir/Effective
medicine or advice

Ilhaam इल्हाम Divine
inspiration/Revelation

Illaa इल्ला If not/
Otherwise/Besides

Iltifaat इल्तिफ़ात Love
and affection/Regard/
Civility/Consideration/
Attention/Courtesy/
Kindness/ Friendship

Iltijaa इल्तिजा Prayer/
Request/Supplication/
Petition/Entreaty

Iltizaam इल्तिज़ाम Being
necessary or expedient

Imdaad इम्दाद Help/
Support/Assistance/
Donation/Favour/
Subsidy/Aid/Relief/
Kindness

Imkaan इम्कां Possibility

Imshab इम्शब Tonight

Imtiyaaz
इम्तियाज़Discernment/
Distinction/
Prominence/Sense/
Judgement/Preference/
Discrimination

Inaayat इनायत Kindness/
Favours

Inaayat-e-bejaa इनायत-
ए-बेजा Inappropriate or
out of place kindness or
reward

Inab इनब Grapes

Indimaal इंदिमाल Cure

Infiaal इंफ़ियाल
Embarrassment/
Contrition/Penitence/
Shame

Inhisaar इन्हिसार Reliance/
Being surrounded/
Encircled

Inkisaarii इंकिसारी
Humbleness/Modesty

Inkishaaf इन्किशाफ़
Discovery

Inquilaabaat-e-dahar
इन्क़िलाबात-ए-दहर
Changes/revolutions/
vicissitudes of the world

Intihaaen इन्तिहाएं
Extremes

Intikhaab इंतिख़ाब
Selection/Election/
Excerpt(from a
book,etc)/Compilation

Intiqaal इंतिक़ाल Death/ Migration/Transfer

Intiqaam इन्तिक़ाम Revenge

Intisaab इन्तिसाब Lineage/ Descent/Relationship/ Connection/Dedication (of a book, etc)

Intishaar इंतिशार Dispersion/Confusion/ Anxiety/Spreading abroad

Iqaamat इक़ामत Stay/ Permanent residence/ Staying/Dwelling/ Lodging

Iqbaal इक़बाल Good fortune/Admission/ Confession/Prosperity/ Luck/High position/ Power/Worldly grandeur/Blessing/ Auspiciousness

Iqraar इक़रार Promise/ Consent/Pledge

Iqtibaas इक़्तिबास Quotation/Citation/

Asking/Begging/ Extraction/Deriving/ Obtaining

Iram इरम Paradise

Irfaan इरफ़ान Wisdom/ Enlightenment

Irfanii इफ़र्ानी Enlightening/ Enlightened

Irshaad इशर्ाद Command/ Guidance

Irtibaat इर्तिबात Affinity

Irtibaat-e-salaasil इर्तिबात- ए-सलासिल Connection of chains

Irtibaat-e-shikan इर्तिबात- ए-शिकन Breakage of bond or friendship

Isbaat इस्बात Affirmation/ Confirmation/ Verification/ Recognition/Establishing

Ishaarat इशारत Coquetry/ Meaningful gesture

Ishaaraton इशारतों Gesticulation/Hint/ Allusion/Indication/ Mark/Pointing to

Ishrat इश्रत Pleasure/ Delight/Enjoyment/ Happiness

Ishtiaal इश्तिआल Burning

Ishtiyaaq इश्तियाक Longing

Ishtiyaaq-e-huur इश्तियाक़-ए-हूर Desire for a beautiful woman

Ishva इश्वा Coquetry/ Blandishment/Ogling/ Amorous playfulness

Ishva-e-but इश्वा-ए-बुत Coquetry/ Blandishments/Ogling/ Playulness of idol

Ism इस्म Denomination/ Appellation/Noun/ Name of a person, place or thing/Repeated recitation of any name of Allah/Sin

Ismat इस्मत Modesty/ Maidenhood

Ismatein इस्मतें Honours/ Modesty (pl)/ Maidenhood

Istiaara इस्तिआरा Metaphor/Simile/ Borrowing/To take a loan/To seek a loan

Istifaada इस्तिफ़ादा To gain advantage or profit or gain/Profit/Gain/ Advantage/Benefit

Istiqbaal इस्तिक़बाल Reception/Welcoming a visitor

Istikhara इस्तिख़ारा Seek the good/Asking Allah to help make the choice between two

Istikhwan इस्तिख़्वान Bone

Isyaan इस्यां Sin

Itaab इताब Anger/Reproach/ Reprimand/Rebuke/ Temper/Displeasure

Itaab-e-muluuk इताब-ए-मुलुक Anger of the rulers

Ittihaad इत्तिहाद Union/ Alliance/Concord/ League/Treaty/ Unification/Friendship/ Amity

Ittisaal इत्तिसाल Conjunction/Union/ Confluence

Izaarband इज़ारबंद Waist band

Izaafil इज़ाफ़िल Additional/ Extra/Over and above/ Supplementary/ Relative/Genitive

Izn इज़्न Permission/ Order/Leave/ Injunction/Consent of two contracting parties

Izn-e-aam इज़्न-ए-आम General permission

Izn-e-khiraam इज़्न -ए-ख़िराम Permission to promenade

Iztiraab इज़्तिराब Restlessness

Izzat-e-saadat इज़्ज़त-ए- सआदत Respectable/ Respectability

J

Yaarab hazaar saal salaamat rahen huzuur
Ho roz jashn-e-iid yahaan jaavedaan basant
Muneer Shikohabadi

Do chaar baras jitne bhii hain jabr hii sah len
Is umr men ab ham se bagaavat nahiin hotii
Akram Mahmud

Ghaas men jazb hue honge zamiin ke aansuu
Paanv rakhtaa huun to halkii sii namii lagtii hai
Saleem Ahmed

Baad muddat ye jilaa kis ke hunar ne bakhshii
Baad muddat mire aaiine men chehre aae
Bakul Dev

Lachak hai shaakhon men jumbish havaa se phuulon men
Bahaar jhuul rahii hai khushii ke phuulon men
Ameer Minai

Haal meraa bhii jaa-e-ibrat hai
Ab sifaarish raqiib karte hain
Hafeez Jaunpuri

Jahl-e-khirad ne din ye dikhaae
Ghat gae insaan badh gae saae
Jigar Moradabadi

Ham jaur-paraston pe gumaan tark-e-vafaa kaa
Ye vahm kahiin tum ko gunahgaar na kar de
Hasrat Mohani

Dhuundtii phirtii hai mutrib ko phir us kii aavaaz
Joshish-e-dard se majnuun ke garebaan kii tarah
Faiz Ahmad Faiz

Jalaa ke mishal-e-jaan ham junuun-sifaat chale
Jo ghar ko aag lagaae hamaare saath chale
Majrooh Sultanpuri

J

Jaa जा Space/Place/Occasion

Jaa-bajaa जा-बजा Here and there/Everywhere

Jaabar जाबर Tyrant

Jaada जादा Manner/Custom/Mode/Road/Route/Pathway

Jaa-e-guzar जा-ए-गुज़र Place for passing/Road/Way

Jaa-e-ibrat जा-ए-इब्रत To take warning from/An occasion to be an example

Jaahil जाहिल Illiterate/Uncouth/Ignorant

Jaama-e-ehraam जामा-ए-एहराम Pious garb of pilgrim on pilgrimage to Mecca

Jaam-e-sifaal जाम-ए-सिफाल Clay cup

Jaam-e-tahuur जाम-ए-तहूर Allusion to nectar in heaven/Sacred drink of paradise

Jaan-bar जान-बर A saviour/Being safe

Jaan-e-nisaar जान-ए-निसार Devoted

Jaan-fazaa जान-फ़ज़ा Life-invigorating/Refreshing/Revitalising

Jaan-gusil जान-गुसिल Heart-breaking/Deadly/Life killer/Tormentor of life

Jaanib जानिब Direction/ Towards/In the direction of/Party or person as a side in a dispute or agreement

Jaan-navaaz जान-नवाज़ Offering life

Jaan-nisaar जान-निसार Devoted/Fervent

Jaan-sitaan जान-सितां Tyrant on life/Beloved

Jaruub जरूब Sweeper/ Broom

Jaaruub-kash जरूब-कश Scavenger/Sweeper/ Janitor

Jaavedaan जावेदां Eternal/ Everlasting/Perpetual

Jaa-ba-jaa जा-ब-जा Everywhere

Jabiin-e-niyaaz जबीन-ए- नियाज़ Praying forehead

Jabr जब्र Force

Jafaa जफ़ा Oppression/ injustice/Infidelity

Jahaan-e-kharaab जहां-

ए-ख़राब World of problems

Jahl जहल Ignorance/ Foolishness/Silliness/A war of words/ Disputation

Jahl-e-khirad जहल-ए- ख़िरद Ignorant of reason or wisdom

Jalaal जलाल Grandeur/ Majesty/Splendour/ Glory/Intensity/ Velocity/Acceleration/ Intensity/Awe

Jallad जल्लाद Executioner

Jalva-farma जल्वा-फ़र्मा Highlighted/Grant and appearance

Jalva-gar जलवा-गर Present/Manifest

Jalaali जलाली One with ferocious anger

Jamaal-e-kam-numaa जमाल-ए-कम-नुमा Less revealing beauty

Jamaali जमाली Beautiful

***Jamhuuriyat* जम्हूरियत**
Democracy

***Jamhuuriyat-navaaz*
जम्हूरियत-नवाज़**
Democrat/Rewarding
democracy

***Jaraahaton* जराहतों**
Surgeries/Incisions

***Jaraasiim* जरासीम** Bacteria

***Jaras* जरस** Bell rung to
signal the departure of
a caravan/Sweet voice/
Humming sound/Bell
on camel's neck

***Jasaaras* जसारस** Boldness/
Courage

***Jasarrat* जसर्रत** Courage/
Bravery/Daring/
Boldness/Fearlessness

***Jast* जस्त** Leap/Bounce/
Jump

***Jasta-jasta* जस्ता-जस्ता**
Eclectically/Selectively/
From here and there

***Jauhar* जौहर** Extract/
Essence/Concentrate/
Jewel/Gem

***Jaulaan-gaah* जौलान-गाह**
Arena

***Jaur* जौर** Tyranny/Cruelty/
Oppression/Violene/
Inconstancy

***Jaur-parast* जौर-परस्त**
Worshippers of tyranny

***Javaahir-khaana* जवाहिर-
खाना** Jewel House

***Javaaz* जवाज़** Lawfulness/
Permit/Permission/
Justification/Legality/
Propriety/Validity

Javed Eternity

***Jazaa* जज़ा** Reward/
Compensation/
Punishment/Revenge/
Blessing/Good return/
Requital

***Jazb* जज़्ब** Absorption/
Allurement/Magnetism/
Attraction/Assimilation

***Jazba* जज़्बा** Spirit/
Emotion/Passion/
Feeling

***Jazb-e-dil* जज़्ब-ए-दिल**
Absorption of heart

Jazb-e-mohabbat जज़्ब-ए-मोहब्बत Absorption in love

Jazb-e-zaruurat जज़्ब-ए-ज़रूरत According to need

Jazbon जज़्बों Spirits

Jaziira जज़ीरा Island

Jhadiyaan झड़ियाँ Constant rain/Drizzle

Jhatka झट्का Killing of an animal for food by cutting off its head in one stroke (as opposed to Muslim way of slaughter)

Jigar-chaak जिगर-चाक Torn heart

Jigar-kharaash जिगर-ख़राश Heart-rending

Jihat जिहत Direction/Side/ Facet/Reason/Account/ Direct

Jilaa जिला Shining

Jism-e-uryaan जिस्म-ए-उरियाँ Nude body

Joban जोबन Bloom/Youth

Johd जोहद Struggle

Josh-e-ashq जोश-ए-अश्क़ Surge of tears

Josh-e-qadah जोश-ए-क़दह Warmth of a goblet

Joshish जोशिश Fervour/ Enthusiasm/Exuberance

Judaagaana जुदागाना Separate

Jumbish जुम्बिश Motion/ Agitation/Vibration/ Jerk

Junuun-sifaat जुनून-सिफ़ात Frenzied qualities

Jurrat-e-rindaana जुर्रत-ए-रिंदाना Courage of a drunkard

Juu जू Rivulet/Canal/ Stream/Source of spring/Seeking/ Seeker

Juu-e-shiir जू-ए-शीर River of milk/Performing an impossible task

Juun जूं As/Which

Juuebaar जूएबार Ravine/ Source of rivulet or spring/Place where there are many ravines and canals

Juz जुज़ Part/Portion/ Ingredient/(In binding) Signature/Folded form(of book)/Part of a book with 8/16 pp

Juzv जुज़्व Besides/Except/ Other than/Part

K

Chaahiye khud pe yaqiin-e-kaamil
Hausla kis kaa badhaataa hai koii
Shakeel Badayuni

Rihaa kar de kafas kii qaid se ghaayal parinde ko
Kisii ke dard ko is dil men kitne saal paalegaa
Aitbar Sajid

Kaisii kashish hai ishq ke tuute mazaar men
Mela lagaa huaa hai hamaare dayaar men
Jitendra Mohan Sinha Rahbar

Judaaiyon kii khalish us ne bhii na zaahir kii
Chhupaae apne gam-o-iztiraab maine bhii
Aitbar Sajid

Ranj se khuugar huaa insaan to mit jaataa hai ranj
Mushkilen mujh par padiin itnii ki aasaan ho gaiin
Mirza Ghalib

Khayaal lams kaa kaar-e-savaab jaisaa thaa
Asar sadaa kaa bhii mauj-e-sharaab jaisaa thaa
Abrar Azmi

Is mahfil-e-kaif-o-mastii men is anjuman-e-irfaanii men
Sab jaam-ba-kaf baithe hii rahe ham pii bhii gae chhalkaa bhii gae
Asrarul Haq Majaz

Shifaa maujuud thii us kii nazar men har maraz kii so
Karishma-saaz ham ko dekh le biimaar kahte the
Siddharth Saaz

Husn-e-be-parvaa ko khud-biin o khud-aaraa kar diyaa
Kyaa kiyaa main ne ki izhaar-e-tamannaa kar diyaa
Hasrat Mohani

Jo kushuud-e-kaar-e-tilism hai vo faqat hamaaraa hii ism hai
Vo girah kisii se khulegii kyaa jo tirii jabiin kii shikan men hai
Haneef Akhgar

K

Kaakh काख़ Palace/
Castle

Kaakh-e-umaaraa काख़-
ए-उमारा Palace of the
rich

Kaamil क़ामिल Full/
Entire/Complete/
Perfect/Mature/
Expert/Thorough/
Accomplished

Kaamraan कामरान
Successful/Lucky

Kaar-e-numaayaan कार-
ए-नुमायाँ Bold action/
Prominent action

Kaar-e-pukhta-kaaraan
कार-ए-पुख़्ता-कारां
Work of mature
experts

Kaar-e-savaab कार-ए-
सवाब Deed which
deserves an award/
Virtuous deed

Kaar-farmaaii कार-
फ़रमाई Doing

Kaar-gaah-e-dahar कार-
गाह-ए-दहर Workshop or
factory of the world/Toil
place of the world

Kaasa कासा Goblet/
Begging bowl

Kaasa-e-muraad कासा-ए-
मुराद Bowl of desire or
wish

Kaashaane काशाने House

Kaatib क़ातिब Writer

Kaatib-e-vaqt कातिब-ए-
वक़्त Writer of time

Kaav काव Concave/
Sunken/Depressed/
Digging/Excavating/
Examining/Investigating

Kaavish काविश Effort/
Endeavour/Search/
Research/Inquiry/
Animosity/Rancour/
Disputing/Fighting/
Enmity/Menacing

Kaazib क़ाज़िब Liar/
Mendacious/False/Fake

Kabk-e-darii क़ब्क-ए-दरी
Species of partridge
found in the hills

Kaf कफ़ Palm

Kafas क़फ़स Prison

Kaf-e-dast-nigaaraan
कफ़-ए-दस्त-निगारां Palm
of hand painted/Painted
palm (with henna)

Kafiil कफ़ील A security/
Pledge/One who
supports/A person
who stands as a surety/
Protector

Kahkashaan कहकशाँ
Galaxy/Milky Way

Kaif कैफ़ Pleasure/Ecstasy

Kaifiyat कैफ़ियत
Rapture/Ecstasy/
Enjoyment/Condition/
Circumstances/
Narrative/Situation/
Quality

Kaifiyat-e-iztiraab
कैफ़ियत-ए-इज़्तिराब
Condition of restlessness

Kaif-o-mastii कैफ़-ओ-
मस्ती Ecstasy and
intoxication

Kaj कज Awry/Crooked

Kajii कजीCrookedness/
Perversity/Raw

Kalaam कलाम Word/
Speech/Conversation/
Talk

Kaliid कलीद Key

Kaliim कलीम Speaker

Kaliimii कलीमी Quality of
conversing with God/
Vision or sight of God

Kaliisa कलीसा Church

Kalma कलमा Muslim confession of faith/ Word/Saying/Part of speech

Kamaal कमाल Perfection/ Completion/Complete/ Culmination/Limit/ Height

Kam-aazaar कम-आज़ार Less annoyance or vexation or molestation or injury

Kamiin-gah कमीं-गह A lurking pace for ambush

Kam-nasiibii कम-नसीबी Less fortunate

Kam-nigahii कम-निगाही Dim-sighted/Short-sighted/Miserliness/ Acrimony/Ignorance

Kam-sin कमसिन Young/ Tender/Beautiful

Kam-zarf कम-ज़र्फ़ Mean/ Vile/Silly

Kamzor-tar कमज़ोर-तर Weaker

Kanaar-e-subh-e-fardaa कनार-ए-सुबह-ए-फ़र्दा Edges of horizons of tomorrow morning

Kaniiz कनीज़ Slave-girl/ Maid servant/Female devotee

Karam-farmaa करम-फ़र्मा Kind person

Karb कर्ब Anguish/ Affliction/Agony/ Grief/Distress

Karda कर्दा Executed/ Effected/Made/Done

Kardanii कर्दनी Feasible/ Practicable/Workable/ Fit to be done/Work/ Deeds/(Something)worth doing/Fit to mke or do

Kariim करीम Bountiful/ Gracious/Merciful/ Epithet of God

Karishmaat-e-tasavvur करिश्मात-ए-तसव्वुर Miracle of imagination

Karishma-saaz करिश्मा-साज़ Charismatic

Kasak कसक Pain/Affliction/Pang/Regret/Lassitude and aching (premonitory of fever)/Dragging or breaking pain (in limbs)

Kashaakash कशाकश Dilemma/Brawl/Squabble/Struggle/Grief and pain/Stretching and straining

Kashaan कशां Walking leisurely/Dragging/Drawing/Attracting/Bearing/Carried/Withdrawing

Kashiid कशीद Brewing/Extraction/Distillation/Derivation/Grief/Sorrow/Moaning/Dragging/Drawing/Pulling

Kashish कशिश Attraction/Allurement/Pull/Drawing power

Kashkol कश्कोल Bowl/Bottom of a pitcher/Wallet/Beggar's bowl

Kaund कौंद Dazzle/Dazzling light/Brightness

Kaundan कौंदन Dazzling flash of light

Kaun-o-makaan कौन-ओ-मकान World/Creation/Universe

Kausar कौसर Lake or river in paradise/Heavenly spring

Kenchulii केंचुली Skin of snake which is sloughed off

Khaak ख़ाक Dust

Khaaka ख़ाका Plan/Outline/Layout/Sketch/Trace/Caricature

Khaak-aagushta-ba-khuun ख़ाक-आगुश्ता-ब-ख़ून Dust mixed woth blood

Khaakistar ख़ाकिस्तर Ashes/Cinder

Khaak-nashinon ख़ाक-नशीनों Ascetics

Khaaksaari ख़ाक़सारी Humility/Modesty

Khaaksaaron ख़ाकसारों Low/Poor/Humble

Khaal-o-aariz ख़ाल-ओ-आरिज़ Mole and cheek

Khaala ख़ाला Vacuum/Space/Hollowness/Lacuna/Absence/A vacant speace or place

Khaam ख़ाम Raw/Unripe/Green/Crude

Khaama ख़ामा Pen

Khaana-badar ख़ाना-बदर Exiled from home/Homeless

Khaana-barbaad ख़ाना-बर्बाद Ruined house

Khaanqaah ख़ानक़ाह Monastery

Khaanumma ख़ानुम्मा Family/House/Home/Household goods

Khaanamaan-barbaad ख़ानमान-बर्बाद Ruined/Miserable/Desolated/Unfortunate

Khaanumaan-kharaab ख़ानुमा-ख़राब Wretched/Broken/Vanquished-hearted/Ruined/Broken-hearted/Anguished

Khaar ख़ार Thorn

Khaar-e-guluu ख़ार-ए-गुलू Thorn in the throat

Khaashaak ख़ाशाक Dry grass

Khaatam ख़ातम Last/Ring/Seal/Stamp with inscription

Khaatir-shikanii ख़ातिर-शिकनी Breaking of admiration or regard

Khabtii ख़ब्ती Crazy/Obsessed/Lunatic/Mad/Foolish/Distorted mind

Khadang ख़दंग Small arrow/Tip of arrow/Poplar from which arrows are made

Khadang-e-jasta खदंग-ए-जस्ता Arrow in flight/ Arrow just shot

Khadbadaae खड़बड़ाए Boiled/Simmered/ Bubbled

Khafaqaan ख़फ़क़ान Palpitation/Fluttering/ Hysteria/Asphyxiation/ Oppression/Supression

Khaafii ख़ाफ़ी Concealed/Hidden Imperceptible

Khaftaan ख़फ़्तान Dress worn over tunic/Ves worn under armour/Caftan

Khair ख़ैर Goodness/ Safety/Better/Good/ However it may be/It is just as well/No mater/ Very well

Khair-o-shar ख़ैर-ओ-शर Good and evil/Virtue and sin

Khair-khvaahon ख़ैर-ख़्वाओं Well-wishers

Khairaat ख़ैरात Charity

Khajiil ख़जील Embarrass/ Abashed/Ashamed/ Penitent/Shame/ Shyness/Bashfulness

Khajista ख़जिस्ता Lucky/ Blessed

Khal ख़ल Skin

Khalaa ख़ला Vacuum

Khalaahon ख़लाओं Spaces

Khaliil ख़लील True and sincere friend/Name of Prophet Abraham

Khalish ख़लिश Misgiving/ Unease/Anxiety/Worry/ Prick

Khalq ख़ल्क़ Creation/ People/Mankind

Khalvat ख़ल्वट Isolation/ Seclusion/Solitude/ Privacy/Private/ Retirement/Retiring room or cell

Khamiida ख़मीदा Bent

Khanda-has-e-gul ख़ंदा-हस-ए-गुल Breaking into laughter of flower

Khanda-zan खंदा-ज़न Setting up a laugh/One who sets up a laugh

Khandaq ख़ंदक़ Moat/Ditch/Pit/Trench

Khanvatii ख़नवती Hermit/Recluse

Khas ख़स Weak/Helpless

Khasaraa ख़सरा Loss/Damage

Khas-o-khaashaak ख़स-ओ-ख़शाक Straw and dried leaves/Sticks and sprigs

Khashaak ख़शाक Dry eaves/Trash/Rubbish

Khasta ख़स्ता Fragile/Wounded/Broken/Sickness/Injured/The state of being wounded or injured

Khastagii ख़स्तगी Weariness/Exhaustion/Fatigue/Wounded state/Infirmity

Khasta-e-teg-e-sitam ख़स्ता-ए-तेग़-ए-सितम Weak from the sword of tyranny

Khatkaa खटका Anxiety/Apprehension/Fear/Dread/Bolt

Khatna ख़त्ना Circumsicion/To separate/To cut/Woman and man's vulva and penis/Tradition in which Muslims circumcise their sons on the 8th day of life

Khatt-e-nafs ख़त्त-ए-नफ़्स Pursuit of sensuality

Khatt-o-khaal ख़त्त-ओ-ख़ाल Features/Shape/Physique

Khauf-e-fasaad-e-khalq ख़ौफ़-ए-फ़साद-ए-ख़ल्क़ Fear of riot of humanity

Khavaas ख़वास Elite/Special/Peculiarities/Specialists/Favourite courtiers and attendants

Khayaabaan ख़याबां
Flower bed

Khayaal-e-roz-e-jazaa ख़याल-ए-रोज़-ए-जज़ा
Notion of the day of doomsday or day of rewards

Khazinon ख़ज़ीनों Treasury

Khez ख़ेज़ Evoking/Giving rise to

Khilat ख़िलट Robe of honour

Khiraaj ख़िराज Paying obeisance/Tribute/Tax/Duty/Impost

Khiraam ख़िराम Graceful walk

Khirad ख़िरद Wisdom/Reason/Intellect/Judgement/Understanding

Khirad-mandii ख़िरद-मंदी Rationality

Khirman ख़िर्मन Harvest/Heap or stock of the unthrashed corn

Khisht ख़िश्त Bricks

Khissat ख़िस्सत
Miserliness/Stinginess/Parsimony/Meanness/Despicable/Being mean/Of low level

Khitaab ख़िताब Title/Address/Conversation/Speech

Khizaab ख़िज़ाब Dyeing/Tingeing hair and nails/Dye/Tincture

Khizar खिज़र Immortal

Khizr ख़िज्र Prophet/Guide

Khosha-chiin ख़ोशा-चीन
Recipient of benefaction

Khosha-e-gandum ख़ोशा-गंदूम Sheaf of wheat

Khubaan ख़ुबाँ Beauties/Sweethearts/Excellence/Virtue

Khud-aaraa ख़ुद-आरा Self-adorer/Arrogant

Khudaagahii ख़ुदागही Self-awareness

Khudaaiyaan ख़ुदाइयां Claims of being God

Khud-aaraa ख़ुद-आरा Self-adorer

Khudaayaan-e-saabit-e-sayyar ख़ुदायाँ-ए-साबित-ए-सय्यार God of fixed and movable

Khud-biin ख़ुदबीं Self-conceited/Proud/Vain

Khuddaam ख़ुद्दाम Servants

Khudii ख़ुदी Ego/Self-esteem

Khud-navisht ख़ुद-नविश्त Autobiography

Khud-raftagii ख़ुद-रफ़्तगी Drunkenness/Intoxication/Senseless/Madness/Automated

Khud-sar ख़ुद-सर Stubborn/Arrogant/Obstinate/Headstrong

Khufta ख़ुफ्ता Hidden

Khulaasa ख़ुलासा Apparent/Evident/Summary/Explanation

Khulaasa-e-ilm-e-qalandri ख़ुलासा-ए-इल्म-ए-क़लंदरी Inference or revelation or explanation or summary of science of asceticism or mysticism

Khuld ख़ुल्द Paradise

Khuluus ख़ुलूस Sincerity/Integrity/Purity

Khur ख़ुर Cloven hoof/Act of eating

Khurd ख़ुर्द Young

Khurd-saal ख़ुर्द -साल Underage

Khurshiid ख़ुर्शीद Sun

Khuruus ख़ुरूस Domestic cock/The person who has more desire for lust/Sensualist

Khushaamad ख़ुशामद Flattery

Khush-aasaar ख़ुश-आसार Good Signs

Khush-fahm ख़ुश-फ़हम Optimist/Fanciful/One who looks at the bright side/Midconceived

Khush-fahmi ख़ुश-फ़हमी Good imagination

Khush-imkaanii ख़ुश-इम्कानी Optimism

Khushk ख़ुश्क Dry

Khush-kalaam ख़ुश-कलाम Well-spoken/ Happy conversation

Khush-khiraam ख़ुश-ख़िराम Good gait/Good walk

Khush-o-khurram ख़ुश-ओ-ख़ुर्रम Cheerful/ Happy

Khush-qad-o-qaamat ख़ुश-क़द-ओ-क़ामत Elegant height and stature

Khuu ख़ू Habit/Custom/ Disposition/Behaviour/ Sweat

Khuubaan ख़ूबां Beauties/ Fair ones/Sweethearts/ Goodness/Virtue

Khuugar ख़ूगर Accustomed/Habituated

Khuun-bar ख़ून-बार Oozing blood/Shedding tears of blood

Khuun-chakaan ख़ून-चकां Blood oozing out/Dripping blood/ Bleeding/Blood-drenched

Khuun-khvaar ख़ून-ख़्वार A beast of prey/Blood thirsty/Beastly

Khuun-rez ख़ून -रेज़ Bloody/Cut throat/ Murder

Khvaab-e-adam ख़्वाब-ए-अदम Death

Khvaab-e-giraan ख़्वाब-ए-गिरां Deep/sound sleep/Unconscious/ Indifference

Khvaab-gaah ख़्वाब-गाह Bedroom

Khvaabiidaa ख़्वाबीदा Sleepy/Drowsy

Khvaah ख़्वाह Wishing/ Desiring/Soliciting/ Willing/Requiring/ Wanting

Khvaahaan ख़्वाहां Desirous/Candidate

Khvaan ख़्वां Reciter/ Reader

Khvaar ख़्वार Shame/ Dishonour/Disgrace/ Abject/Wretched/ Miserable/Distressed/ Ruined Worried/ Confounded/Perplexed/

Khvaarii ख़्वारी Contemptibleness/ Meanness/Vileness/ Abjectness/ Wretchedness/Distress

Khyaal-e-pukhta ख़्याल-ए-पुख़्ता Firm belief/ Thought

Kibr किब्र Pride/Grandeur

Kiimiyaagar कीमियागार Alchemist

Kiina कीना Malice/ Rancour/Grudge/ Enmity

Kiina-saaz कीना-साज़ Mean

Kinaaya किनाया Allusion/ Innuendo

Kingra किंगरा Parapet/ Pinnacle/Turret/Crest

Kirchen किरचें Shards/Pieces

Kirdaar किरदार Character/ Deed/Conduct/Manner

Kisht किश्त Instalment/ Sown field

Kisht-e-viiraan किश्त-ए-वीरान Deserted field

Kishvar किश्वर Empire/ Territories

Koh कोह Mountain

Koh-e-nidaa कोह-ए-निदा Voice of mountain

Koh-e-qaaf कोह-ए-क़ाफ़ Caucasian Mountains/A lonely or inaccessible place/Abode of giants and fairies

Koh-e-tuur कोह-ए-तूर Mountain where Moses saw the divine light

Kohkan कोहकन Mountain digger

Kohsaar कोहसार Range of mountains/Mountainous country

Kotaahii कोताही Deficency/Want/ Brevity/Narrowness

Kuduurat कुद्रत Enmity/ Resentment/Meenness/ Ill-will

Kul कुल Whole/All/Entire/ Aggregate/Each and every thing/ Complete/ Family/ Tribe/ Lineage/ Pedigree

Kulaah कुलाह Hat/Cap/ Headgear/Bonnet

Kulliyaat कुल्लियात Complete works

Kuhan कुहन Ancient

Kuhan-saal कुहन-साल Aged

Kuhna कुहना Ancient/ Old/Obsolete

Kun-fayaakuun कुन-फयाकून 'To be' or 'to exist' and 'it is'

Kunj कुंज Secluded or solitary place/Confined space/Corner/

Kushaa कुशा Airiness/ Openness

Kushaada कुशादा Wide/ Ample/Open/Spacious/ Uncovered/Expanded/ Free/Frank/Loose

Kushta कुशता Martyr/ Residue after calcification/One desperately in love/ Killed/Slain

Kushtagaan कुश्तागां The one's desperately in love/ the slain/Those who have been killed

Kushton कुश्तों Those killed

Kushuud-e-kaar-e-tilism कुशूद-ए-कार-ए-तिलिस्मOpener/Revealer of talisman

Kuu-ba-kuu कू-ब-कू Everywhere/From place to place/From street to street

Kuulhaa कूल्हा Hip/ Buttock

Kuuza-gar कूज़ा-ग़र Potter

L

Tuk dekh len chaman ko chalo laala-zaar tak
Kyaa jaane phir jien na jien ham bahaar tak
Meer Hasan

Dil vo hai ki fariyaad se labrez hai har vaqt
Ham vo hain ki kuchh munh se nikalne nahiin dete
Akbar Allahabadi

Lahad men kyuun na jaauun munh chhupaae
Bharii mahfil se uthvaayaa gayaa huun
Shad Azimabadi

Lauh-e-jahaan pe is tarah likkhaa gayaa huun men
Jis kaa koii javaab nahiin vo savaal huun
Khaleel Tanveer

Jhuut bhii sach kii tarah bolnaa aataa hai use
Koii luknat bhii kahiin par nahiin aane detaa
Zafar Sahbai

Abas hai sochnaa laa-intihaa ke baare men
Nigaahen kyuun na jhukaa luun jo aasmaan dekhuun
Sagheer Malal

Badal chukaa hai miraa lams nafsiyaat us kii
Ki rakh diyaa hai use main ne an-chhuaa kar ke
Ali Zaryoun

Miltii hai gam se ruuh ko ik lazzat-e-hayaat
Jo gam-nasiib hai vo badaa khush-nasiib hai
Vafa Malikpuri

Kabhii ai haqiiqat-e-muntazar nazar aa libaas-e-majaaz men
Ki hazaaron sajde tadap rahe hain mirii jabiin-e-niyaaz men
Allama Iqbal

Ye taaza-kaarii hai tarz-e-ehsaas kaa karishma
Mire lugat men to lafz koii nayaa nahiin hai
Irfan Sattar

L

Laa-davaa ला-दवा Incurable

Laag लाग़ Spite

Laagarii लाग़ारी Leanness/ Deficiency of virility/ Weakness

Laa-intihaa ला-इंतिहाInfinite

Laa-mutanaahii ला-मुतनाही Infinite

Laal-o-gohar लाल-ओ-ग़ौहर Rubies and pearls

Laala लाला Tulip

Laala-o-gul लाला-ओ-गुल Tulips and flowers/ Beauty/Freshness/ Greenery/Pretty/Beloved

Laala-azaar लाला-आज़ार Tulip (red) cheeked

Laala-zaar लाला-ज़ार Bed of roses

Laam लाम Greed/Avarice

Laa-mahduud ला-महद्दूद Unlimited/Unbounded

Laa-makaan ला-मक़ान Deity/Without place or abode

Laa-ubaalii ला-उबाली Careless/Reckless/ Devil-may-care/ Insolent

Laazim-o-malzuum लाज़िम-ओ-मलज़ूम Connected with one another

Lab-e-gor लब-ए-ग़ोर On the verge of death/Near death

Lab-e-goyaa लब-ए-गोया
Speaking lips

Lab-e-juu लब-ए-जू Shore
of a river

Labrez लबरेज़
Overflowing/Brimful

Lagaavat लगावट
Attachment/Adherence/
Intimate connection/
Intimacy/Closeness/
Liason/Sexual intercourse/
Affection/Love

Lagan लगन Pans

Laghzish लग़्ज़िश Blunder/
Error/Shake/Tremble/
Shiver/Slippery/
Slipping/Sliding/
Stumbling/Falling

Laghzish-e-paiham
लग़्ज़िश-ए-पैहम
Constant trembling

Lahad लहद Cavity where
dead body is kept in a
grave

Lahza लहज़ा A moment/A
minute/A glance/Wink
of an eye

Lahza-ba-lahza लहज़ा-
ब-लहज़ा Moment by
moment

Lail-o-nahaar लैल-ओ-
नहार Night and day/
Times/Circumstances

Lailatul-qadr लैलतुल-क़द्र
Night of power (27th
night of Ramadan when
the Q'ran began to be
revealed to the Prophet
of Islam

Lakht लख़्त Piece/
Bit/Portion/Part/
Little/Continuously/
Immediately

Lams लम्स Sense of touch/
Touch/Tactile sense

Laqab लक़ब Appellation of
honour/Title/Epithet/
Name in which qualities
of a person are
known

Larzish लर्ज़िश Quivering/
Shivering

Lashkar लश्कर Army/
Encampment

Lauh लौह Tablet/Plank/ Board on which one writes

Lazzat-e-hayaat लज़्ज़त-ए-हयात Enjoyment or pleasure or relish of life

Lek लेक But/Still/Yet/ Nevertheless

Libaadon लिबादों Apparel

Libaas-e-majaaz लिबास-ए-मजाज़ Latent or unmanifest apparel

Lobaan लोबां Frankincense/Resin burnt for its smell

Lugaat लुग़ात Dialect/ Language/Words/ Dictionary/Modes oif writing and pronouncing words

Luknat लुक्नत Stammer/ Stammering/Stuttering

Lutma लुटमा Injured

M

Zindagii shama kii maanind jalaataa huun 'nadiim'
Bujh to jaauungaa magar subah to kar jaauungaa
Ahmad Nadeem Qasmi

Sarak kar aa gaiin zulfen jo in makhmuur aankhon tak
Main ye samjhaa ki mai-khaane pe badlii chhaaii jaatii hai
Nushur Wahidi

Ham se shaayad motabar thahrii sabaa
Jis ne ye gesuu sanvaare aap ke
Ibn-e-Mufti

Havaa to hai hii mukhaalif mujhe daraataa hai kyaa
Havaa se puuchh ke koii diye jalaataa hai kyaa
Khurshid Talab

Muntazir huun main kafan baandh ke sar se 'aajiz'
Saamne se koii khanjar nahiin aayaa ab tak
Ajiz Matvi

Jahaan maabuud thahraayaa gayaa huun
Vahiin suulii pe latkaayaa gayaa huun
Rais Amrohvi

Ise ham-raah paataa huun ye saae kii tarah meraa
Taaaqub kar rahaa hai jaise main mafruur mulzim huun
Akhtarul Iman

Kitnaa achchhaa thaa ki ham bhii jiyaa karte the 'faraaz'
Gair-maaruuf se gumnaam se pahle pahle
Ahmad Faraz

Zaabte aur hii misdaaq pe rakkhe hue hain
Aaj-kal sidq-o-safaa taaq pe rakkhe hue hain
Gulzar Bukhari

Kaisii bastii thii jahaan par koii bhii aisaa na thaa
Munkashif main jis pe kartaa apne dil kii baat ko
Shahryar

M

Maaal मआल End/Result/
Consequence/Place of
refuge/Place of return/
Termination

Maaal-e-dahar मआल-ए-
दहर End of the world

Maaanii-khez मआनी-ख़ेज़
Giving rise to meaning/
Producing meaning

Maaash मआश
Subsistence/Livelihood

Maaaz मआज़ Shelter/
Refuge/At the mercy of/
In the protection of/Safe
place/Secure place

Maabuud
माबूदWorshipped/
Adored

Maadar-e-dahr मादर-ए-
दहर Mother of world or
time/Eternity

Maaduum मअद्म Extinct/
Non-existent/Absent/
Annihilated/Wanting/
Not found/Not existing

Maail माइल Inclined/
Bent/Attracted

Maajraa माजरा State/
Condition/Incident/
Happening

Maal-o-zar-e-divaar-o-dar
माल-ओ-ज़र-ए-दीवार-
ओ-दरWealth and gold
of walls and doors/
Property

Maamuure मामूरे Thriving

Maandagii मांदगी
Tiredness/Fatigue/
Indisposition/Illness

Maane माने Hindrance/ Bar/Impedimet/Barrier/ Preventing/Forbidding/ Obstructing

Maanii-khez मायनीखेज़ Evoking meaning/ Meaningful/Significant

Maaniind मानींद Just as/ Like/Resembling

Maanuus मानूस Associated/Familiar (with)/Attached/ Friendly/Intimate/ Used to/Well-known/ Companion

Maarkaa मार्का Victory/ Place or scene of battle/ Battle-ground/Fight/ Strife

Maarke मार्के Battles/ Expeditions/ Adventures/ Contests

Maaaash मआश Subsistence/Livelihood

Maaaz मआज़ In the protection of/At the mercy of/Safe place/ Secure place/Shelter

Maaaz-allah मआज़-अल्लाह I seek the protection of God/ Heaven defend me/At the mercy of God/God forbid/Vowing to sin no more/Repentance/ Renunciation

Maandagii मांदगी Fatigue/Weariness/ Indisposition/Illness

Maashii माशी Black

Maatar मातर Accustomedness

Maa-siva मा-सिवा Besides/ Moreover/Over and above/Apart from/ Other than/ Except

Maaya-e-naaz माया-ए-नाज़ Wealth that is a cause of pride

Maazarat मअज़रत Excuse/Apology/Plea

Maazii माज़ी Past

Maazi-e-marhuum माज़ी-ए-मरहूम Dead past

Maazuul मअज़ूल Suspended

Maazuur मअज़ूर Helpless/Disabled

Mabaadaa मबादा God forbid/Lest/Let it not be/Never/Perchance/May it not be/Be it not/By no means

Madaar मदार Axis/Pivot/Basis/Centre

Madfan मद्फ़न Tomb/Grave

Madfuun मद्फ़ूं Interred/Buried/Concealed/Hidden/Underground (as treasure)

Madfuun-e-dariya मद्फ़ूं-ए-दरिया Water-burial

Madh मद्ह Eulogy/Praise

Mafruur मफ़रूर Absconding

Magas मगस Honey-bee

Magfirat मग़फ़िरत Remission/Forgiveness/Absolution/Deliverance/Salvation/Pardon

Magmuum मग़मूम Sad/Afflicted/Grieved/Sorrowful

Magrib मग़रिब West/Sunset/Sundown/Evening/Sunset prayer/Europe and Western countries

Magruur मग़रूर Proud

Magz मग्ज़ Brain/Cerebra/Kernel/Chief substance or essence of anything/Intellect

Mah मह Moon

Mahaaba महाबा Love/Romance

Mahaar महार Bridle/Rein

Mahbas महबस Prison/Confinement/Jail/Lock-up/Prisoner/Jailed/Locked-up

Mahbuus महबूस Prisoner/ Captive/Confined/ Frenzied/Detained/ Arrested/Jailed/ Incarcerated/Tied

Mahbuus-e-rasan महबूस-ए-रसन Tied with ropes/ Confined

Mahduud महद्दूद Limited/ Restricted

Mah-e-siyaam मह-ए-सियाम Moon of Ramzan

Mahi महि Fish

Mahjuur महजूर Lovelorn/ Foresaken/Rejected/ Cut-off/Separated/ Forbidden/Prohibited/ Prevented

Mahkuum महकूम Slave/ Servant/Subject/The ruled/Subjugated/Under control

Mah-laqaa मह-लक़ाMoon-faced

Mahmil महमिल Camel's litter/Saddle of camel

Mah-o-anjum मह-ओ-अंजुम Moon and stars

Mahr महर Sun

Mahram महरम Confidant

Mahruum महरूम Deprived

Mahshar महशर Judgement day/Doomsday/Tumult

Mahshar-e-khayaal महशर-ए-ख़्याल Pandemonium of thoughts/Bedlam

Mahsuul महसूल Tax/ Custom/Octroi/Excise

Mahv महृ Absorbed/ Fascinated

Mahaviiyyatein महवीय्यतें Absorption/Being totally lost in thought

Mah-e-daagii मह-ए-दाग़ी Bemished moon

Mah-e-shavval मह-ए-शव्वल 19th Islamic month which comes after Ramadan/Eid-ul-Fitr comes on first of Shavval

Mahram महरम Forbidden/ Prohibited/Anyone admitted to women's apartments/Women's relative to whom marriage is forbidden and before whom she may appear unveiled

Mahruum महरूम Deprived of/Debarred/ Excluded/Refused

Mahruum-e-inaayat महरूम-ए-इनायत Deprived of reward

Mahshar महशर Place of assembly or congregation/Tumultous place/Commotion by the elegance of a sweetheart's gait

Mahtaab महताब Moon

Mah-vash मह-वश Moon-faced

Mahzuun महज़ून Melancholy/ Melancholic/Grieved/ Afflicted/Sorrowful/ Distressed

Mahzuuz महज़ूज़ Delighted/Pleased

Mai-e-naab मइ-ए-नाब Near wine

Mai-kash मय-कश Drinkers

Majaaz मजाज़ Competent/ Lawful/Authorised/ Legally authorised

Majaazii मजाज़ी Metaphorical/ Figurative/Unreal/ Illisive/Feigned/ Insincere

Majlisii मज्लिसी Social

Majma मजमा Horde/ Congregation

Majmuua मजमुआ Collection

Majrooh मजरूह Wounded/Bruised/ Smitten/Injured/Hurt

Makaan मकां Space/House

Makhluut मख़लूत Mixed

Makhmuur मख़्मूर Intoxicated

Makharab मख़रब Spoiler

Makhsuus मख़सूस
Specified/
Distinguished/Special/
Reserved/Private

Makiin मकीं Dweller/
Resident/Inhabitant/
Inmate/Settler

Makr मक्र Deceit/
Cheating

Maktab मक़तब School

Maktuub मक़तूब Letter/
Epistle/Written/
Message/Writing/
Collection of letters/
Sewn or stiched
or pasted together
collection of letters

Makun मकुन
Do not

Malaamat मलामत
Reproach/Rebuke/
Reprehension/Censure/
Blame/Humiliation/
Denounce/Reproof/
Accusation/Blame/
Disgrace/Opprobium

Malak मलक Angel/Divine
messenger

Malbuus मलबूस Clothes/
Clothed/Garments

Maluul मलूल Sad/
Dejected/Melancholy/
Weary

Mamaat ममात Death

Mamnuun मम्नू Obliged/
Thankful/Grateful/
Beholden

Maane-e-parvaaz माने-
ए-परवाज़ Hindrance to
flight

Manauub मनऊब
Related(to)/
Connected(with)/
Attributed/Ascribed/
Referred to/Betrothed/
Engaged for marriage/
Fiance/Appointed/
Nominated/Fixed/
Related to manifestation

Mansoor मंसूर Victorious

Mansuub मंसूब Appointed/
Nominated/Fixed/
Related to manifestation

Mansuur मंसूर Succoured/ Helped/Triumphant/ Victorious

Mantiq मंतिक़ Discourse

Manzar मंज़र Sight/View

Manzar-e-shab-taab मंज़र-ए-शब्-ताब Scene of bright light

Manzil-e-gamnaak मंज़िल-ए-ग़मनाक Tragic destination

Manzil-e-ibrat मंज़िल-ए-इबरत Exemplary destination

Manzil-e-maqsuud मंज़िल-ए-मक़सूद Aim/Goal/ Destination

Manzuum मंज़ूम Versified/ Metrical/In verse form/ Arranged in order/ Joined/Threaded/Strung

Maqaam मक़ाम Place/ Position/Occasion/ Dwelling

Maqaam-e-khatar मक़ाम-ए-ख़तर Dangerous spot

Maqaamaat मक़ामात Ranks/Places

Maqaamaat-e-gum-shudaa मक़ामात-ए-गुम-शुदा Unknown places

Maqbool मक़बूल Accepted/ Chosen/Received/ Pleasing

Maqduur मक़दूर Means/ Resources/Power/ Ability/Authority

Maqluub मक़लूब Inverted/ Reversed/ Palindrome

Maqmuur मक़मूर Sad

Maqsuud मक़सूद Intended/ Proposed/Beloved/ Intent/Object/Aim/ View/Target/Design

Maqtaa मक़ता Last couplet of a ghazal which often contains the takhallus

Maqtal मक़तल Place of slaughter

Maraahil मराहिल Stages

Maraasim मरासिम Relationships/Customs/Rules/Regulations/Usages/Dealings/Relations

Mardum मर्दुमPeople/Folk/Man/Civil/Humane/The pupil of an eye

Marg मर्ग़ Death

Marg-e-naa-gahaanii मर्ग़-ए-ना-गहानी Sudden or untimely death

Marhabaa मरहबा Greeting/Welcome/Hail/Bravo

Marhale मरहले Stage

Markab मरक़ब Anything in which one is carried

Marmar मर्मर Marble

Martaba मर्तबा Degree/Office/Rank/Status/Turn/Time/Class/Account/Order/Step/Station/High rank/Post of honour

Maruub मरऊब Awe-struck/Overawed/Impressed

Maruuf मरऊफ Famous

Masaafat मसाफ़त Journey/Distance/Interval/Period/Time/Space

Masaaib मसाइब Plural of musiibat/Calamities/Misfortunes/Miseries/Discourse on the sufferings of the Karbala martyrs

Masaail मसाइल (Metaphorically) problems/Questions/Propositions/Precepts/The precepts of Prophet Mohammed

Masaail-e-tasavvuf मसाइल-ए-तसव्वुफ़ Problems of mysticism

Masal मसल Like/For example/Proverbial/Adage/Saying/Maxim

***Masarrat* मसर्रत**
Happiness/Joy/
Pleasure/Cheerfulness/
Rapture/Delight/
Gladness

***Masduud* मस्दद** Closed/
Shut/Obstructed/
Stopped

***Mashaam* Fragrance/
Organ of smell/Smell/
Sense of smelling

***Mashaqqat* मशक़्क़त**
Labour/Pain/Toil/
Trouble

***Mashghala* मशग़ाला** Hobby/
Pastime/Occupation/
Vocation

***Mashiyyat* मशिय्यत**
Pleasure/Will/Wish/
God's will/Fate

***Mashkiiza* मश्कीज़ा** Small
leather bag for carrying
water

***Mashq* मश्क़** Exercise/
Practice/Drill

***Mashq-e-sukhan* मश्क़-ए-
सुख़न** Drill of poetry

***Maskh* मस्ख़** Distorted/
Misshapen/Deformed/
Mutilation/Camouflage

***Masiih* मसीह** Blessed/
Sincere/Massaged with
oil/(Metaphorically)
lovely/Pretty/Beloved

***Masiihaa-nafas* मसीहा-
नफ़स** One who's breath
is as effective as the
breath of Christ/Expert
doctor

***Masjuud* मस्जूद** Adored/
God/To whom one
bows or worships

***Maskh* मस्ख़** Distorted/
Deformed/Misshapen/
Mutilation

***Maskon* मस्कों** Sycophancy/
Butter

***Maslahat* मस्लहत** Prudent
measure/Prudence/
Policy/Good thing/
Expedience/Usefulness/
Convenience/
Advisability/Diplomacy

Maslahatan मस्लहतन Hidden reason

Masruur मस्रूर Glad/ Cheerful/Delighted/ Happy/Pleased/Joyful

Mass-e-havaa मस्स-ए-हवा Touch of breeze

Mast-e-zuhuur मस्त-ए-जुहूर Intoxicated by manifestation

Mastuur मस्तूर Concealed/ Hidden/Covered/ Veiled/Written/ Expressed

Mataa मताअ Capital/ Commodity/Assets/ Property/Possessions/ Goods/Valuables/ Merchandise

Matlaa मतला Opening rhyming couplet of a ghazal/East/Place of rising sun/Both lines of the matlaa contain the qaafiya and radif

Matlab मत्लब Meaning/ Motive/Aim

Matluub मतलूब Desired/ Longed for/That which is sought/Demanded

Matn मत्न Text

Mauhuumii मौहूमी Imagined/Fancied/ Supposed

Mauj-e-havaadis मौज-ए-हवादिस Waves of calamity

Maujzan मौज्ज़न Tumultous/Stormy/ Exciting

Mauquuf मौक़ूफ़ Dependent on/Depend upon/Suspended/ Potponed/ Delayed/ Deferred/ Stopped/ Abolished/Dismissed/ Ceased/Stopped/Based on

Mausam-e-saffaaq मौसम-ए-सफ्फाक़ Cruel season

Mausuuf मौसूफ़ Praised/ Celebrated/Aforesaid

Mauzuu मौज़ू Subject/ Topic/Object

Mauzuu-e-guftuguu मौज़ुअ-ए-गुफ़्तगू Topic of conversation

Mauzuu-e-sukhan मौज़ुअ-ए-सुख़न Topic of conversation/Title of poetry

Mauzuun मौज़ूँ Proper/ Apt/Fit/Appropriate/ Suitable/Well-adjusted/ Well-balanced/ Weighed/Metrical

Mayaar मयार Quality

Mayyat मय्यत Corpse/A dead body

Mazaa-daar मज़ा-दार Entertaining

Mazaahib मज़ाहिब Religions

Mazaamiin मज़ामीन Essays/Articles

Mazaazii मज़ाज़ी Figurative/Metaphorical

Mazhar मज़्हरManifestation/ Phenomenon

Mazkuur मज़्कूर Expressed/Mentioned/ Recorded/Related/ Mention/Said/ Remembered/Aforesaid

Mazluum मज़्लूम Injured/ Oppressed/Wronged/ One who is wronged

Mazmuun मज़मून Essay/ Article/Subject/ Objective/Topic/ Purport/Sense/Context/ Subject matter

Mearaaj मेअराज Ladder/ Ascension

Mehdii मेहदी Leader/Guide/ One who is led in the right way/12th Imam who is still living as per Shia belief

Mehfil-e-khubaan महफ़िल-ए-ख़ुबान Assembly of beauties

Mehraab मिहराब Pricipal niche in the mosque from where the imam conducts prayers/ Arched niche/Arches

Mehr-e-darakhshaan मैहर-ए-दरख़्शां Bright sun

Mehrii मैहरी Head-stall/ That part of a bridle that encompasses the head

Mehr-o-mah मैहर-ओ-मह Sun and moon

Mehr-o-vafaa मैहर-ओ-वफ़ा Love and fidelity

Mehvar मैहवर Axis/ Center/Axle

Memaar मेमार Mason/ Architect/Builder/ Inventor/Founder/ Leader

Meraaj मेराज Ladder/ Ascension

Meraaj-e-mustafaa मेराज-ए-मुस्तफ़ा Ascension of the Prophet

Meyaar मेयार Standard measure or weight/ Touchstone/Yardstick

Meyaarii मेयारी Qualitative/Standard/Of good standard

Mid-hat मिदहत Eulogy/ Praise/Commendation

Miim मीम Shape

Miiraas मीरास Estate/A bequest/Ancestral/ Property/Heritage

Miiraas-e-pidar मीरास-ए-पिदर Heritage of father

Miir-e-kaarvaan मीर-ए-कारवाँ Leader of caravan

Miirzaaii मीरज़ाई Princedom/Gentility/ Pride/Nobles/Prices/ Children of Mughals

Miisaaq मीज़ाख़ Covenant/ Treaty

Miizaan मीज़ां Scale

Milk-o-maal मिल्क-ओ-माल Country/Wealth

Millat मिल्लत Community

Mimbar मिंबर Pulpit

Minnat-kash मिन्नत-कश Desirous/Obliged

Minnat-kash-e-davaa मिन्नत-कश-ए-दवा Obliged to medicine

Minnat-kash-e-sahra मिन्नत-कश-ए-सहरा Desirous of desert

Mirg मिर्ग Death

Misdaaq मिस्दाक़ Proof/Evidence/Testimony

Mishal मिशल Light/Beacon

Misii मिसी Lip colouring substance

Miskin मिस्किन Understate/Less speech

Misl-e-baada-khvaar मिस्ल-ए-बादा-ख़्वार Resembling a drunkard

Misl-e-habaab मिस्ल-ए-हबाब Resembling a bubble

Mismaar मिस्मार Demolished/Razed

Missii मिस्सी Powder used for tinting the teeth black

Mistar मिस्तर Pages with ruled lines/Foot rule

Mizgaan मिज़गां Eye lashes

Moajaza मोअजज़ा Miracle

Moajize मोअजीज़े Wonders/Miracles

Moallim मोअल्लिम Teacher

Moattar मोअत्तर Perfumed/Fragrant/Scented

Mohkam मोहकम Firm/Strong/Stable/Fortified/Clear/Incontrovertible/Unequivocal/Verse of Quram whose meaning is clear/Unambiguous/Clear/Lasting/Stable/Solid

Mohmal मोहमल Obsolete/Meaningless

Mohmil मोहमिल Not governing/Unpointed/Spoken without meaning

Mohtaat मोहतात Cautious

Mohtasib मोहतसिब Supervisor of observance of law and punishment

Mominaan-e-saadiq मोमिनां-ए-सादिक़ True believer

Mongiyaa मोंगिया Of the colour of red coral

Motabar मोतबर Reliable/ Trustworthy

Motadil मोतदिल Moderate

Motaqid मोतक़िद Adherent/Believer in faith, creed or person/ Faithful servant/Friend

Motarif मोतरिफ़ A confessor/One who acknowledges or confesses/Confessing

Muamme मुअम्मे Puzzles/ Riddles/Crosswords

Muayyan मुअय्यं Fixed/ Established/Definite

Mubaahise मुबाहिसे Arguments/Discussion

Mubaalge मुबालगे Exaggerations/ Hyperboles

Mubaashir मुबाशिर One who lies with a woman for sex/One who commences or undertakes an affair

Mubaddal मुबद्दल Altered/ Changed/Exchanged/ Substituted

Mubham मुबहम Ambiguous/Equivocal/ Dubious/Doubtful/ Hidden/Indistinct

Mubtala मुब्तला Engaged/ Afflicted/Entangled/ Involved/Busy

Mudaam मुदाम Eternal/ Perpetual/Everlasting/ Permanently/ Eternally

Mudaaraat मुदारात Courtesy/Politeness/ Hospitality

Mudaava मुदावा Cure

Mufiid मुफ़ीद Beneficial/ Useful/Profitable/ Advantageous

Muflis मुफ़्लिस Poor

Muftiyon मुफ़्तियों Expounders of Muhammadan law

Mugaan मुगां Tavern-keeper/Spiritual guide

Mugannii मुग़न्नी Singer

Mugbacha मुगबचा Boy serving wine in a tavern

Mugiilaan मुगीलां Babool/ Acacia

Mugtanim मुगतनिम Opportune/ Advantageous/ Worthwhile

Muhib-e-vatan मुहिब-ए-वतन Patriot

Muhiit मुहीत Encircling/ Surrounding/ Circumambient/ Encompassing/ Enclosing/Periphery/ Containing/ Embracing/ Knowing/Well-acquainted(with)/ Ocean/Sky/One who comprehends/That which (or he who) surrounds or contains

Muhiit-e-be-karaan मुहीत-ए-बे-करां Encompassing shoreless space

Mujrimaana मुजरिमाना Criminal/Cuplable

Mujrimaan-e-ishq मुजरिमाँ-ए-इश्क़ Delinquent or guilty of love or ardour

Mukaafat मुक़ाफ़त Retaliation/Retribution/ Nemesis/Recompense/ Requital

Mukaafaat-e-amal मक़ाफ़ात-ए-अमल Recompense of deed(especialy misdeeds)/ Compensation of deeds

Mukhaalif मुख़ालिफ़ Opposite/Enemy/ Unfavourable/An opponent

Mukhaalifat मुख़ालिफ़त Contravention/ Breach/Conflict/ Dispute/Infringement/ Obstruction/ Opposition/Hostility/ Repugnance/ Contradiction/ Transgression/ Dissension

Mukhtaar मुख़्तार
Competent/Authorised/
Legally empowered

Mukhtaari मुख़्तारी
Independence/Power/
Authority

Mukhtalif मुख़्तलिफ़
Different

Mukhtatam मुखततम
Finished/Completed

Mukhtsar मुख़्तसर Brief

Mulhid मुल्हिद Atheist/
Unbeliever/Heretic/
Pagan/Infidel

Mulk-e-baqaa मुल्क-ए-बक़ा
The afterlife

Muluuk मुलूक Ruler

Mumkina मुमकिना
Possible

Munaajaat मुनाजात
Prayer/Invocation/
Hymn/Supplication to
God/Whispering/Secret
conversation

Munavvar मुनव्वर
Illuminated/Lustrous/
Radiant/Bright

Mundril मुन्द्रिल Ear-ring/
Stud

Munfaiil मुंफ़इल Ashamed/
Abashed/Bashful

Munhadim मुन्हदिम
Demolished

Munhasir मुन्हसिर
Dependent(on)/Resting
(on)/Besieged/Limited/
Confined/Surrounded

Muniir मुनीर Shining

Munim मुनिम Benefactor/
Donor/Grantor/Rich/
Generous/Wealthy/
Liberal

Munjamid मुंजमिद
Frozen/Congealed/Set/
Solid/(metaphorically)
senseless or inactive

Munkashif मुन्कशिफ़
Discovered/Revealed/
Disclosed/Manifest

Munkir मुंकिर Non-believer/
To deny or retract

Munkir-e-ghalib मुंकिर-ए-
ग़ालिब One who denies
greatness of Ghalib

Munsalik मुन्सलिक
Joined/Threaded/
Strung (as in beads)/
Enrolled (in)/Joined/
Appended/Annexed/
Filed (as papers)/Added
(metaphorically)/Being
drawn into (as in one
thing into
another)

Munsif मुंसिफ़ Judge/
Arbitrator/Just/
Equitable

Muntakhab मुन्तख़ब
Chosen/Selected/
Choice/Select/
Rare/(politics)
elected

Muntashir मुंतशिर
Spread/Dispersed/
Diffused/Propagated/
Divulged/Distracted or
bewildered/ Scattered/
Published

Muntazir मुन्तज़िर
One who waits/
Expectant

Muqaabil मुक़ाबिल
In front(of)/In
comparison(with)/
Face-to-face/Opposite/
Converse/Confronting/
Comparing/Matching/
Comparing (with)/
In opposition (to)/
Opposing

Muqaam मुक़ाम
Dwellin/Place/
Position/
Occasion

Muqaddam मुक़द्दम Above
all/Antecedent/Chief/
Prior

Muqaddas मुक़द्दस
Holy/Sanctified/
Consecrated

Muqaffal मुक़फ़्फ़ल Lock/
Locked

Muqarrar मुक़र्रर
Pre-determined/
Established/Fixed/
Repeating/Recurring/
Repeatedly/Encore/
Once more

Muqattaaat मुक्त्तआत Initial letters of some Quranic verses/Short poems or verses/Small cuttings(of cloth)/Narrow strips(of cloth)/Bits or parts or portions/Texts(of scripture)

Muqiim मुक़ीम Inhabitant/Residing/Fixed/Stationed

Muraasalaat मुरासलात Correspondence

Muraqqa मुरक्क़ा Album/Portfolio

Murassaa मुरस्सा Written in rhyming and grandiose words/Studded with jewels & precious stones

Murassa-saaz मुरस्सा –साज़ Jeweller/Inlayer/Stone setter

Murattab मुरत्तब Arranged/Compiled/Set in order/Classified

Muravvat मुरव्वत Kind-heartedness/Affection/Humanity/Respect/Regard/Deference/Indulgence

Murdaar मुर्दार Squalid/Impure/Ugly/Corpse/Carrion/Profane/Obscene/Dead animal not halal

Murda-shuu मुर्दा-शू Washer of dead bodies

Murgaan मुर्गाँ Birds

Murgh मुर्ग़ Cock/Bird

Muriid मुरीद Disciple

Murtasim मुर्तसिम One who sketches or draws/Printer/Engraver/Writer

Musaahib मुसाहिब Close friend/Comrade/Associate/Companion/Courtier

Musaavaat मुसावात Equality/Parity/Evenness/Equation/Indifference/Laziness/Sloth

Musalla मुसल्ला Prayer mat

Musalsal मुसलसल
Constant

Musavvir मुसव्विर Painter/
Sculptor/Photographer

Musavvarii मुसव्विरी
Painting/Photography

Mushahida मुशाहिदा
Witnessing/
Contemplation

Mushavvash मुशव्वश
Disturbed/Perplexed/
Embroiled/Intricate

Mushk-e-shab-e-taar
मुश्क-ए-तब-ए-तारMusk
of dark night

Mushtaaq मुश्ताक़Longing
for/Desirous/Eager/
Yearning/Longing

Mushtahar मुश्तहर
Advertised/Announced/
Proclaimed

Mustahiq मुस्तहिक़
Deserving

Mushtail मुश्तैल Excited/
Inflamed/Kindled/
Blazing

Mushtamil मुश्तमिल
Containing/Comprising/
Including/Inclusive
(of)/Comprehending/
Encompassing/
Extending over

Mushtaqbil मुश्तक़बिल
Future/Future tense

Mushtarak मुश्तरक
Common/Joint

Musht-e-ustukhvaan
मुश्त-ए-उस्तख्वां Mere
skeleton/Very weak
body

Musir मुसिरInsistent/
Adamant/Unyielding

Mustaaar मुस्तार
Borrowed/Obtained or
taken as a loan

Mustafa मुस्तफ़ा Chosen/
Select/A title for
Prophet Muhammad

Mustahkam मुस्तहकम
Firm/Stable/
Established/Strong/
Regulated(Electronics)

Mustanad मुस्तनद
Authentic/Reliable/
Confirmed/
Authoritative/Certified/
Incontrovertible

Mustaqil मुस्तक़िल
Persistent/Assiduous/
Consistent/Fixed/
Permanent/Firm/
Stable/Constant/
Enduring/Durable/
Unshaken/Unshakable

Mustarad मुस्तरद Reject

Mutaala मुताला Study

Mutaalba मुताल्बा
Demand/Claim/
Requirements/Due/
Requisition/Exaction

Mutassir मुतअस्सिर
Affected/Impressed/
Influenced/Impacted/
Worried/Sad/Suffering

Mutlaq मुत्लक़ Wholly/
Altogether/Universal/
Absolute

Mutlaqan मुत्लक़न
Absolutely/Entirely

Mutmain मुत्मैन Satisfied

Mutrib मुतरिब Singer

Muttafiq मुत्तफ़िक़
Agreeing/Consenting/
United

Muttasil मुत्तसिलAdjoining/
Joined/Contiguous/
Continual/
Uninterrupted/
Successive/In an
unbroken line

Muu-e-aatish मू-ए-आतिश
Hair that has seen fire/
Singed hair

Muu-e-dost मू-ए-दोस्त
Beloved's hair

Muvaafaqat मुवाफ़क़त
Accord/Agreement/
Concord/Conformity/
Consonance/Affinity/
Correspondence

Muyassar
मुयस्सरFacilitated/
Feasible/Practical/
Favourable/Rendered
easy

***Muzayyan* मुज़य्यन**
Adorned/Decorated/
Embellished/Bedecked

***Muzhda* मुज़दा** Good
news/Good tidings

***Muzmahil* मुज़महिल**
Infirm/Weak/Fatigued/
Exhausted/Sad/
Anguished/Stressed/Idle

***Muzmar* मुज़मर** Concealed/
Latent/Hidden

***Muzmoon* मज़मूं** Essay/
Subject

***Muztar* मुज़्तर** Distressed/
Afflicted/Anxious/
Troubled

***Muztarib* मुज़्तरिब**
Afflicted/Agitated/
Uneasy/Confused/
Restless

N

Ham khud bhii hue naadim jab harf-e-duaa niklaa
Samjhe the jise patthar vo shakhs khudaa niklaa
Hilal Fareed

Gam-o-nashaat kii har rahguzar men tanhaa huun
Mujhe khabar hai main apne safar men tanhaa huun
Makhmoor Saeedi

Chalo lahuu bhii charaagon kii nazr kar denge
Ye shart hai ki vo phir raushnii ziyaada karen
Manzoor Hashmi

Goggle lagaa ke aankh par chalne lage hasiin
Vo lutf ab kahaan nigah-e-niim-baaz kaa
Hashim Azimabadi

Har qadam duuri-e-manzil hai numaayaan mujh se
Merii raftaar se bhaage hai bayaabaan mujh se
Mirza Ghalib

Apnii naamuus kii aatii hai hifaazat jin ko
Jaan de dete hain dastaar nahiin dete hain
Abdushshukoor Aasi

Nigaah-e-lutf mat uth khuugar-e-aalaam rahne de
Hamen naakaam rahnaa hai hamen naakaam rahne de
Asrarul Haq Majaz

Niim-shab chaand khud-faraamoshii
Mahfil-e-hast-o-buud viiraan hai
Faiz Ahmad Faiz

Shab kii bahaar subh kii nudrat na puuchhiye
Kitnaa hasiin hai khvaab-e-mohabbat na puuchhiye
Shakeel Badayuni

Phir us ke baad kaii log uth ke jaane lage
Main uth ke jaane kaa nuskha bataa ke baith gayaa
Zubair Ali Tabish

N

Naa-ahal ना-अहल
Incapable/Unfit/
Unworthy

Naa-biinaa ना-बीना
Blind

Naachaar नाचार
Helpless

Naadim नादिम Repentant/
Ashamed/Contrite/
Apologetic

Naaf नाफ़ Navel

Naa-gahan ना-गहन
Unexpected/Accidental

Naa-gufta ना-गुफ़्ताUnsaid/
Untold

Naa-hamvaar ना-हमवार
Dishevelled/Uneven

Naa - haq ना-हक़ Uncalled
for/Unjust

Naa-karda ना-करदा
Not done

Naa-khush-andeshii
ना-ख़ुश-अंदेशी Lack of
ideas/Lack of advises/
Pessimism

Naama नामा
Letter/Book/
History/Treaty

Naama-bar नामा-बर
Messenger

Naama-o-paighaam
नामा-ओ-पैग़ाम Exchange
of letters or messages/
Correspondence/Letter
and message

Naam-o-nasab नाम-
ओ-नसब Name and
descent/Lineage

Naa-muraadii ना-मुरादी
Disappointment/ Failure/Misfortune

Naamuus नामूस Chastity

Naamvar नामवर
Renowned/Celebrity/ Well-known/Celebrated

Naa-padiid ना-पदीद Concealed/ Invisible/Hidden

Naaqa नाक़ा
She-camel

Naaqid नाक़िद Critic/ Reviewer/Fault-finder/ Assayer/Scrutiniser

Naaquus नाक़ूस Conch shell

Naar नार Fire/Fibre of which rope is made/ Leather thing/Neck/ Pomegranate/Wife/ Woman/Girl/Neck

Naara नारा Exclamation

Naa-rasaaii ना-रसाई
Inability/Incapacity/ Failure

Naa-rasaaiyon ना-रसाइयों
Not accessible/Beyond reach/Unreachable

Naarasaaon नारसाओं
Beyond reach/ Unreachable

Naara-zanii नारा-ज़नी
Slogan shouting

Naarii नारी Full of fire/ Fiery/Hellish/Woman/ Wife

Naarishwar-e-dauraan नारिश्वर-ए-दौरान Elegance of the times

Naarsa नारसा
Incommunicado

Naashaad नाशाद
Cheerless/Joyless/ Sadness/Sorrow/ Despondency/Woe/ Gloom

Naa-shuniidan ना-शुनीदां
Unheard

Naa-tamaam ना-तमाम
Unfinished/Deficient/ Incomplete/Imperfect

Naavak नावक Arrow

Naavak-e-naaz नावक-ए-नाज़ Arrows of love

Naazaan नाज़ां Proud/Conceited/Arrogant/Exhaggerated sense of one's importance or abilities

Naazil नाज़िल Descending/Alighting/Arriving at/Revealed

Naazish-e-dauraan नाज़िश-ए-दौरान Elegance/Pride/Conceit/Haughtiness/Arrogance/Boasting of the times

Nadaamat नदामत Regret/Self-reproach/Repentance/Shame

Nadaaram नदारम Do not have

Nadiim नदीम Friend/Companion/Favourite courtier of the king/Confidant

Nafas नफ़स Breath/Soul/Spirit/Self

Nafas-e-baaz-pasiin नफ़स-ए-बाज़-पसीन Last gasp of breath

Nafat नफ़त Profit

Nafs नफ़्स Body/Flesh/Sensual appetite/Carnal desire

Nafsiyaat नफ़्सियत Psychology

Nagiina नगीना Gem/Jewel/Precious stone or ring/Anything that fits or sits well

Nagma-e-shaadii नग़मा-ए-शादी Song of happiness

Nagmagii नग़मगी Lyricism

Nagma-saraaii नग़मा-सराई Singing melodies

Nahaar नहार Lunch

Nahang नहंग Alone/Solitary/Free from care/Unconcerned/Naked/Shameless

Nahr-e-furaat नहर-ए-फ़ुरात River Euphrates

Nahv नह्व Path/Mode/Way

Nairang नैरंग Deceit/Trick/Magic/Sorcery/Miracle/Anything new or strange

Najaat नजात Deliverance/Escape/Salvation/Liberation/Absolution/Freedom/Pardon

Najd नज्द A horse found in Najd province of S Arabia/High ground in S Arabia

Najuubiyon नजूबियों Astrologers

Nakh-ba-nakh नख़-ब-नख़ Little by little/Line by line/Row by row/Rank by rank

Nakhchiir नख़चीर Victim/Prisoner/Chase/Hunting/Game/Prey

Nakhl नख़्ल Date tree/Sapling/Tree

Nakhl-e-hirmaan नख़्ल-ए-हिरमान Tree of destiny

Nakhvat नख़्वत Pride/Conceit/Haughtiness

Naksh नक़्श Print/Mark/Impression/Engraving/Charm

Namruud नमरूद A powerful God/One who cast Abraham into the fire/Cruel/Arrogant/Haughty

Nang-e-vajuud नंग-ए-वजूद Shame on existence

Naql-e-makaanii नक़्ल-ए-मकानी Migration/Moving from a place/Removal/Removing

Naqqaaraa नक़्क़ारा Big drums/Voice/Wish

Naqd-o-nisyah नक़द-ओ-निसयाह Cash & credit/Pleasure of the world now vs borrowing the happiness which will be found in the hereafter

Naqs नक़्स Flaw/Blemish/
Diminution

Naqsh नक़्श Ikon/Picture

Naqsh-ba-diivaar नक़्श-
ब-दीवार Like a picture
on a wall/Confounded/
Motionless/Like a statue

Naqsh-e-kaf-e-paa नक़्श-
ए-कफ़-ए-पा Footprints

Naqsh-e-khayaal नक़्श-ए-
ख़याल Imaginary imprint
or painting

Naqsh-e-kuhan नक़्श-
ए -कुहनOld belief/
Custom/Building/
Ancient imprint

Naqsh-e-vafaa नक़्श-ए-
वफ़ा Imprint of love or
constancy

Naqsh-o-nigaar नक़्श-ओ-
निगार Decoration and
embellishment

Nashaat नशात Joy/
Cheerfulness

Nashaat-e-kaar नशात-ए-
कार Ecstatic

Nasheb नशेब Slope/
Descent

Nasheman नशेमन Nest

Nashtar नश्तर Lancet/
Cutter

Nashv-o-numaa नश्व-ओ-
नुमा Growth/Increase

Nasiim नसीम Light or
gentle breeze

Nasiyaan नसियान
Forgetfulness

Natwaan नतवां Impotent

Nauj नौज God forbid/
On no account/By no
means

Nau-khez नौ-ख़ेज़
Youthful/Young/Newly
sprung up/Adolescent

Nauha नौहा Plaintiveness/
Lamentation/Requiem/
Dirge

Nauha-e-gam नौहा-ए-ग़ाम
Dirge of sorrow

Nauha-gar नौहा-गर
Mourner/Elegy singer/
Wailing

Nauha-garii नौहा-गरी Mourning/Lamenting

Nauha-khvaani नौहा-ख़्वानी Lamenting/weeping

Nau-rusta नौ-रस्ता Fresh/New blooming

Navaa नवा Expression

Navaa-garii नवा -गरी Singing/Chanting

Navaa-saaz नवा-साज़ Musical instrument player

Navaa-sanj नवा-संज One emitting a spound/Playing on music/Singer/Musician/Song

Navaa-sanj-e-fugaan To cry out or to lament

Navaa-sanjii नवा-संजी Singing/Chanting

Navaa-sarosh नवा-सरोश Voice

Navaaz नवाज़ Cherishing/Soothing/Caressing/Playing on music/Performer

Navaazish नवाज़िश Favour/Politeness/Patronage/Kindness/Courtesy

Navardii नवर्दी Wandering

Navishte नविश्ते Letters/Documents/Written/Inscribed/Writing/Fate/Destiny

Nayaab नयाब Rare

Nazar-shanaas नज़र-शनास Knowing/Clever

Naziir नज़ीर Example/Instance/Like

Nazm-e-gulistaan नज़्म-ए-गुलिस्तां Order/Arrangement of the garden

Nazr नज़्र Offering/Gift/Present/Bribe

Nazzaargii नज़्ज़ारगी Spectacle

Neamat नेअमत Gift

Neze नेज़े Spears/Reeds from which pen is made

Nezon नेज़ों Spears/Lances

Nifaaq निफ़ाक़ Discord/ Enmity

Nigaah-e-lutf निगाह-ए-लुत्फ़Glance of love

Nigaar निगार Figure/ Effigy/Portrait/Picture/ Beloved/Idol

Nigaaraan निगारां Painted

Nigaar-e-taabaan निगार-ए-ताबां Radiant beauty

Nigahbaan निगहबान Guard

Nigaah-daarii निगाह-दारी Eye to eye contact

Niguun निगूँ Hanging down/Turned upside down/Inverted/Bent

Niguun-bakhton निगूँ-बख़्तों Those with declining fortunes

Nihaan निहां Hidden

Niim-baaz नीम-बाज़ Half-closed/Intoxicated

Niim-khvaabii नीम-ख़्वाबी Drowsiness/Half-asleep/Dozing/Lethargy

Niim-shab नीम-शब् Midnight

Nikhat निकहतFragrance

Nikhat-e-baad-e-bahaarii Fragrance of spring-breeze

Niqaad निक़ाद Critic

Nisaa निसा Women/ Ladies/Tye female sex

Nisaab निसाब Syllabus/ Curriculum/Course/ Capital/Fortune/ Property

Nisaar निसार Sacrifice

Nisbat निज़्बत Relation/ Affinity/Comparison/ Betrothat/Engagement/ In proportion (to)

Nisbat-e-ishquii निज़्बत-ए-इश्क़ी Relationship of love

Nishast निशस्त Session/ Seat

Nisyaan निस्यां Forgetfulness/Amnesia/ Oblivion

Niyaaz नियाज़ Need/
Desire/Petition/
Supplication/Prayer/
An offering/Thing
dedicated/Humility/
Obedience/Meeting/
Acquaintance

Niyyaz-bandii नियाज़-
बंदी Humbleness/
Obedience/Humility/
Entreaty

Niyaaz-mand नियाज़-मंद
Supplicating/Needy/
Humble/Obedient

Niyyat निय्यत Aim/
Purpose/Intention/
Motive

Niyyat-e-shauq निय्यत-ए-
शौक़ Intention to love

Nizaam निज़ाम System/
Rule/Regulation/
Practice/Order/
Arrangement/Habit/
Custom/Way of life

Nudrat नुदरत Rareness

Nujuum नुजूम Astrology/
Stars/Starlight

Numuu नुमू Growth

Numuud नुमूद
Appearance/Display/
Show/Sight/
Conspicuousness/
Celebrity/Prstige/
Honour

Numuud-e-suvar नुमूद-
ए-सुवर Display of great
patience

Numuudaar नुमूदार
Apparent/Visible/
Conspicuous

Nujuum नुजूम
Stars/Astrology/
Starlight

Nukta-daan नुक़्ता
-दान Discerning/
Subtle/Sagacious/Of
penetrating intellect

Nukta-saraa नुक़्ता -सरा
Connoisseur of fine
nuances/
Appreciator

Nukta-varon नुक़्ता-वरों
Those who understand
nuances

Numaayaan नुमायां Apparent/Prominent/ Visible/Conspicuous/ Salient

Numuud नुमूद Show/ Display/Appearance/ Manifestation/Sight/ Conspicuous/Celebrity/ Honour/Prestige/ Character

Numuudaar नुमूदार Apparent/Conspicuous/ Visible/Sprout/Growth

Numuud-e-aarzoo नुमूद-ए-आर्ज़ू Appearance of desire

Numuud-e-suvar नुमूद-ए-सुवर Growth of great patience

Nuqta नुक़्ता Dot

Nuqta-e-sabz नुक़्ता-ए-सब्ज़ Green dot

Nuquush नुक़ूश Marks/ Features/Picture/ Remains/Relics/Effect

Nur-afshaan नूर-अफ्शां Light diffused

Nuskha नुस्ख़ा Recipe/ Prescription/ Document/Copy (of a book or document)/ Treatise/Edition

Nutq नुत्क़ Power of speech and reasoning/ Articulation/Language

Nuur-badaamaan नूर-बदामाँ Light in hem

Nuurii नूरी Full of light

P

Jab main ne kahaa dil miraa paamaal kiyaa kyuun
Kis naaz se bole ki mohabbat kii sazaa thii
Muztar Khairabadi

Thodaa saa aks chaand ke paikar men daal de
Tuu aa ke jaan raat ke manzar men daal de
Kaif Bhopali

Nafrat bhii usii se hai parastish bhii usii kii
Is dil saa koii ham ne to kaafar nahiin dekhaa
Alamtaab Tishna

Kii tark-e-mai to maail-e-pindaar ho gayaa
Mainn tauba kar ke aur gunahgaar ho gayaa
Dagh Dehlvi

Har aadmii men the do chaar aadmii pinhaan
Kisii ko dhuundne niklaa koii milaa mujh ko
Fuzail Jafri

Jis kii gardan men hai phandaa vahii insaan badaa
Suuliyon se yahaan paimaaish-e-qad hotii hai
Muzaffar Warsi

Mujh men paivast ho tum yuun ki zamaane vaale
Merii mittii se mire baad nikaalenge tumhen
Abhishek Shukla

Us ne to sadaa puuje hain udte hue jugnuu
Vo chaand-sitaaron kaa parastaar hii kab thaa
Qateel Shifai

Jo bhii hain parvarda-e-shab jo bhii hain zulmat parast
Vo to jaaenge usii jaanib jidhar jaaegii raat
Suroor Barabankvi

Isii sabab se to ham log pesh-o-pas men hain
Usii se bair bhii hai aur usii ke bas men hain
Iqbal Umar

P

Paa-ba-giil पा-ब-गील
Restrained/Immobile/
Helpless/
Prisoner

Paabandii-e-rasm-e-fugaan पाबंदी-ए-रस्म-ए-फुगां Restriction of
tradition of crying

Paa-basta पा-बस्ता Stable/
Firm/Established/
Strong/Arrested/Feet
bound

Paaedaar पा-ए-दार
Permanent/Durable/
Steady/Firm

Paaedaarii पा-ए-दारी
Durability

Paa-e-kham पा-ए-ख़म
Bottom of the glass

Paa-e-maal पा-ए-माल
Ruined/Devastated/
Subdued

Paa-e-nigaah पा-ए-निगाह
At a glance

Paaentii पाएनती Foot
of tomb or grave or
bedstead/Towards head

Paakbaaz पाकबाज़
Chaste/Pure/Honest/
Virtuous/Austere/One
who abstains from sin/
Holy

Paamaal पामाल Trodden/
Trampled/Ruined

Paan-khurda पान-ख़ुर्दा
Chewing of betel leaf

Paara पारा Portion/Bit/
Piece/Fragment/Patch

Paara-e-dil पारा-ए-दिल
Piece of heart

Paarsaa पार्सा Pure/
Chaste/Abstemious/
Holy/Virtuous person

Paarsaaii पारसाई Purity/
Chastity/Holiness/Self-
restraint

Paas पास Regard

Paasang पासंग
Counterweight/Balance

Paasbaan पासबां Guard/
Sentinel/Watchman

Passbaan-e-aql पासबां-ए-
अक़्ल Guard of intuition

Paash पाश Breaking

Paash-paash
पाश-पाश
Broken

Paayaab पायाब Shallow/
Fordable (can be
forded)/Within one's
depth/Ford/
Moorage

Pahre पहरे Guard/Watch/
Guarding

*Paighaam-e-hayaat-e-
javedaan* पैग़ाम-ए-
हयात-ए-जावेदां Message
of eternal love

Paiham पैहम Together/
Continuous/
Successively/Close

Paimaaii पैमाई
Measurement/Measure

Paimaaish
पैमाइश Measurement/
Inquiry about the limit
or quality of something/
Measure/Survey (land)/
Measuring

Paimaan पैमान Vow/
Promise

Paikar पैकर Form/
Appearance/Visage/
Figure/Body

Paikar-e-harf-o-sadaa
पैकर-ए-हर्फ़-ओ-सदा The
image of word and
sound

Paikaar पैकार War/Battle/
Contest

Paikaan पैकान Tip of
arrow

Paik-e-tasavvur पैक-ए-
तसव्वुर Arrow of fancy/
Reach of experience

Paiharan पैहरन Dress/
Apparel

Pairaae पैराए Ways/
Methods/Manners/
Styles/Conduct

Paivast पैवस्त Joined/Stuck
together/Pierced

Paivasta पैवस्ता
Contiguous/Joined/
Linked/United/Old/
Clinging close/Sticking
close

Partav पर्तव Ray/Beam/
Light/Splendour/
Shadow/Reflection/
Image

Palang पलंग Cheetah

Panaahgiir पनाह-गीर
Refugee/Asylum seeker/
To hide in a secure
place/The oe who is in
shelter

Par-afshaanii पर-अफ़शानी
Act of flapping the wing

Para-para पारा-पारा In
pieces

Parastaar परस्तार Adorer

Parastish परस्तिश
Worship/Adoration

Paraaganda परागंदा
Disarranged/Disturbed/
Scattered/Distracted

Parda-daar पर्दा-दार Privy

Parda-daarii पर्दा-दारी
Removing the veil/
Revealing the truth/
Fault-finding/Ignominy/
infamy

Par-e-sarhad पर-ए-सरहद
Beyond boundaries

Parizaad परिज़ाद Born of a
fairy/Beautiful

Parkaar परकार Compass/
Decorated/Skillful/Full
of workmanship/Thick/
Wise/Clever

Partav पर्तव Reflection/
Shadow/Image/Light/
Ray/Beam

Partav-e-khur पर्तव-ए-ख़ूर Sun's reflection

Parvarda परवरदा Fostered/Brought up/Nourished

Parvezii पर्वेज़ी Flying/Flight

Pas पस Behind/After

Pas-e-marg पस-ए-मर्ग After death

Pas-e-mohabbat पस-ए-मोहब्बत Regard for love

Pashemaan पशेमां Embarrassed/Penitent/Repentant/Ashamed/Contrite/Remorseful

Pashemaanii पशेमानी Embarrassment

Paziiraaii पज़ीराई Acceptance/Reception/Entertainment/Welcome/The act of accepting/Ovation

Pechdaar पेचदार Complex/Complicated

Pech-o-kham पेच-ओ-ख़म Perplexity/Difficulty

Pesh-e-yaar पेश-ए-यार In front of lover

Pesh-khema पेश-ख़ेमा Prelude/Harbinger

Pesh-o-pas पेश-ओ-पस Vacillation/Indecision

Peshtar पेश-तर Before/Formerly/Prior to/Earlier

Phaag फाग़ Red colour thrown on each other on Holi

Pidar पिदर Father

Piir पीर Holy man/Spiritual guide/Cunning and shrewd man/Founder of a religious order/Old man

Piir-e-kharaabaat पीर-ए-ख़राबात Tavern owner

Piir-e-mugaan Keeper of tavern

Pindaar पिंडार Pride/Conceit/Arrogance/Notion/Thought/Imagination

Pinhaan पिन्हां Concealed/
Hidden

Pistaan पिस्तां Breast

Posh पोश Hide

Poshiida पोशीदा Concealed/
Hidden/Secret/Covered/
Veiled/Secretly/Covertly/
Hunter's trap

Pur-asraar पुर-असरार
Mysterious

Pursish पुर्सिश
Interrogation/Enquiry/
Asking/Questioning/
Visiting the sick

Pursish-e-gam पुर्सिश-ए-ग़म
Asking about sorrow

Pur-soz पुर-सोज़ Burning/
Lighted/Blazing

Pusht-panaahii पुश्त-
पनाही Support/Backing/
Background

Putliyaan पुतलियां Pupils/
Puppets

Q

Qaasid payaam-e-shauq ko denaa bahut na tuul
Kahnaa faqat ye un se ki aankhen taras gaiin
Jaleel Manikpuri

Mire vajuud ke andar hai ik qadiim makaan
Jahaan se main ye udaasii udhaar letii huun
Asima Tahir

Qalaq aur dil men sivaa ho gayaa
Dilaasaa tumhaaraa balaa ho gayaa
Altaf Hussain Hali

Ye ijz hai ki qanaaat hai kuchh nahiin khultaa
Bahut dinon se vo khair-o-khabar se baahar hai
Abul Hasanat Haqqi

Duurii huii to us ke qariin aur ham hue
Ye kaise faasle the jo badhne se kam hue
Unknown

Ham aisii kul kitaaben qaabil-e-zabtii samajhte hain
Ki jin ko padhh ke ladke baap ko khabtii samajhte hain
Akbar Allahabadi

Kaise kaise gile yaad aae 'Khumaar'
Un ke aane se qabl un ke jaane ke baad
Khumar Barabankavi

Qahqaha maarte hii diivaana
Har gam-e-zindagii ko bhuul gayaa
Jaun Eliya

Mire labon se tabassum mazaaq karne lagaa
Main likh rahaa thaa qasiida udaas hone kaa
Rahat Indori

Khud par jo etimaad thaa jhuutaa nikal gayaa
Dariyaa mire qayaas se gahraa nikal gayaa
Bharat Bhushan Pant

Q

Qaabiil क़ाबील
Cruel/Tyrant

Qaabil-e-zabtii क़ाबिल-ए-
ज़ब्ती Liable or deserving
to be seized

Qaafila-saalaar क़ाफ़िला-
सालार Chief of caravan

Qaafiya क़ाफ़िया The
rhyming pattern. The
radif is preceded by
words or phrase with the
same end rhyme pattern
called the qaafiyaa

Qaafiya-paimaaii क़ाफ़िया-
पैमाई Measuring rhyme

Qaail क़ाइल Agreeing/
Consenting/Convince/
Acknowledgement/
Acquiescing/A sayer/An
assertor/Saying

Qaalib क़ालिब Mould/
Frame/Body

Qaamat क़ामत Height/
Stature/Shape/Figure/
Form

Qaasid क़ासिद Messenger

Qabl क़ब्ल Previous(to)/
Before

Qadah क़दह Goblet

Qadah-khvaar क़दह-
ख़्वार Wine drinker

Qadam-bosii क़दम-
बोसी Kissing the feet/
Homage/Obeisance

Qadgan क़दग़न
Injunction/Prohibition

Qadiim क़दीम Old/
Ancient/Traditional

Qadir क़ादिर Powerful/ Almighty/Capable/ Confident/Able/ Potent/Mighty/Havig legal power

Qahba क़हबा Adulteress/ Whore/Prostitute

Qahqaha क़हक़हा Guffaw/ Loud laughter

Qahr क़हर Anger/Rage/ Wrath/Fury/Calamity/ Curse/Violence/ Oppression/Conquering

Qaht क़हत Dearth

Qalandarii क़लंदरी Ascetic/Mystical/Going against the established social or religious norms

Qalaq क़लक़ Regret/ Discomfort/Trouble/ Anxiety/Deep regret/ Sorrow

Qalb क़ल्ब Heart/Main body of the army/Centre of an army/Kernel/ Inverting/Turning/ Winding

Qalbii क़ल्बी Relating to the heart/Heartfelt/ Fake/Counterfeit

Qamar क़मर Moon

Qaleel क़लील Poor/ Scarce/Bare/Meagre

Qanaaat क़नाअत Contentment

Qandeel क़ंदील Lamp/ Lantern/Candlestick

Qariin क़रीं Closely resembling/Fellow/ Member of a society/ Close/Near/Connected/ Friend/Courtesy/ Manners/Etiquette/Way

Qariine क़रीने Decorations

Qariin-e-jaan क़रीन-ए-जां Close to life

Qasaas क़सास Retort

Qasas क़सस Retribution/ Vengeance

Qash-ariiraa कश-अरीरा Horror making hair stand erect/Trembling with fear

Qashqa क़श्क़ा Mark on forehead/Tika

Qasiida क़सीदा A poem in praise of someone

Qasr क़स्र Palace

Qata क़ता To finish

Qat-e-taalluq क़त-ए-तआल्लुक़ Break in relations

Qatl-gaah क़त्ल-गाह Place of slaughter/Abattoir

Qattaala क़त्ताला Slayer/Killer

Qattaalii क़त्ताली Killing/Slaying/Related to murder

Qaul क़ौल Promise/Adage/Word/Speech/Quotation

Qaul-o-qaraar क़ौल-ओ-क़रार Promise and acceptance/Treaty/Mutual agreement

Qaus क़ौस Arch/The area of a circle/Bowl

Qavaa क़वा Body parts

Qayaam क़याम Stay

Qayaas क़यास Presumption/Supposition/Guess/

Qazaa क़ज़ा Fate/Death/Omitted prayer or fast/Lapse/Administration of justice/Judgement/Decree/Divine order/Destiny/Faith/Prayer or fast performed after its actual time

Qaziya क़ाज़िया Tiff/Court case/Judgement

Qibla क़िब्ला Holy mosque at Mecca/Kaaba/Direction to which Muslims bow during prayer

Qibla-e-aalam क़िब्ला-ए-आलम Monarchs of the world

Qibla-numaa क़िब्ला-नुमा Instrument to find direction of Mecca/Compass/Facing west

Qirtaas क़िर्तास Paper/
Canvas/Amulet

Qissa-khvaan क़िस्सा-ख़्वां
Story-teller/Reciter of
tales

Qudsiya कुद्सिया Pure/
Holy

Qufl कुफ़्ल Lock

Qufl-e-abjad कुफ़्ल-ए-
अब्जद A lock with
numbers/A kind of
coded-lock/Puzzle

Qulqul कुलकुल Sound
made by water in the
neck of a bottle while
being poured out/Net
to catch birds/Agile/
Quick/An active man/
Frivolous or nonsensical
talk

Qurb-o-javaar कुर्ब-ओ-
जवार Vicinity/In and
around/Proximity

Quvvat कुव्वत Strength

Quvvat-e-takhayyul
कुव्वत-ए-तख़य्युल Power
of imagination

R

Go raahzan kaa vaar bhii kuchh kam na thaa magar
Jo vaar kaargar huaa vo rahnumaa kaa thaa
Akbar Hameedi

Kyuunkar badhaauun rabt na darbaan-e-yaar se
Aakhir koii to milne kii tadbiir chaahiye
Mardan Ali Khan Rana

Ajiib hii thaa mire daur-e-gumrahii kaa rafiiq
Bichhad gayaa to kabhii laut kar nahiin aayaa
Iftikhar Arif

Zaraa se rizq men barkat bhii kitnii hotii thii
Aur ik charaag se kitne charaag jalte the
Atiiqullah

Umr bhar khul nahiin paate hain rumuuz-o-asraar
Log kuchh saamne rah kar bhii nihaan hote hain
Quaiser Khalid

Gum-shuda tanhaaiyon kii raaz-daan achchhii to ho
Main yahaan achchhaa nahiin huun tum vahaan achchhii to ho
Kafeel Aazar Amrohvi

Rah-e-qaraar ajab raah-e-be-qaraarii hai
Ruke hue hain musaafir safar bhii jaarii hai
Ram Awtar Gupta Muztar

Thii paanv men koii zanjiir bach gae varna
Ram-e-havaa kaa tamaashaa yahaan rahaa hai bahut
Rajinder Manchanda Bani

Kyuun mujhe sangsaar karte ho
Kab ye main ne kahaa rasuul huun main
Abid Munavari

Ai 'mushafii' sad-shukr huaa vasl mayassar
Iftaar kiyaa roze men us lab ke rotab se
Mushafi Ghulam Hamdani

R

Raad राड

Thunder

Raaegaan राएग़ां Useless/
In vain/Fruitless/
Wasted

Raaegaanii राएग़ानी
Uselessness/
Fruitlessness

Raah-e-adam राह-ए-अदम
Last journey/Death

Rahnumaa रह-नुमा
Guide/Leader/Pilot/
Conductor

Raahzan राहज़न Highway
robbers

Raal राल Salliva/Spittle

Raam राम
Tame/Pacified/
Submissive

Raanaaii-e-khayaal
रानाई-ए-ख़्याल Beauty or
elegance or sublimity of
ideas

Raas रास Be suitable

Raasaaii रासाई Access/
Approach/Entrance/
Arriving/Skill/
Acuteness/Sharpness
of mind/Perspicacity/
Reach

Raasha रअशा
Tremor

Raaz-daan राज़-दान
Secret keeper/
Confidant

Raba रबा Quarters

Rabt रब्त Conection/
Relation/Bond/Intimacy

Rabt-e-baahamii रब्त-ए-बाहमी Mutual attachment or attraction

Rabt-e-qalbii रब्त-ए-क़ल्बी Emotional bond/ Intimacy

Rad रद Refund/Echo/ Giving back/Refuse

Radif रदिफ़ Refrain word or phrase. Both lines of the matlaa and the second line of all shers must end with the same refrain

Rafaaqaton रफ़ाक़तों Friendships/ Companionships/ Company

Rafat रफ़त Highness/ Eminence

Rafiiq रफ़ीक़ Friend

Rafta रफ़्ता Past

Rafta-e-raftaar रफ़्ता-ए-रफ़्तार Speed of the bygone ages

Rafta-rafta रफ़्ता - रफ़्ता Slowly/Gradually

Raftagaan रफ़्तगां Those who are dead and gone/ Departed

Rag रग Vein/Artery / Fibre/Nerve/Control/ Authoruty/Feeling/ Emotion/Nature/Habit

Ragbat रग़बत Curiosity/ Interest/Inclination

Rag-e-jaan रग-ए-जां Jugular vein

Rag-e-taak रग-ए-ताक Vines of grape

Rahbar रहबर Guide

Rahbaraan-e-qaum रहबरां-ए-क़ौम Leaders of the nation

Rah-e-qaraar रह-ए-क़रार Way of rest

Rahiim रहीम Merciful

Rahiin रहीं Mortgaged/ Indebted

Rahiin-e-sitam-haa-e-rozgaar रहीं-ए-सितम-हा-ए-रोज़गार Indebted or pledged to the tyrannies of life

Rah-navard राह-नवर्द
Vagrant/Wanderer

Rahnumaa रह-नुमा
Guide/Leader/Pilot/
Conductor

Rahnumaaii रहनुमाई Leadership/
Guidance

Rah-rau राह-रौ Travel
companion

Rah-ravaan राह-रवां
Followers/Fellow
travellers

Rah-ravaan-e-khaak-basar राह-रवां-ए-ख़ाक-बसर Travellers living on
dust

Rah-rav-e-rah-e-iksiir रह-रव-ए-रह-ए-इक्सीर Devoted to the
way of elixir

Rahzan रहज़न
Highwayman/
Robber

Rakaab रक़ाब Stirrup

Rakaat रक़अत Portion of
Islamic prayer

Rakhna-haa-e-siina रख़ना-हा-ए-सीना
Obstacles of the heart

Rakhsh रख़्श Brilliance/
Splendour/Rays or
reflection of life/Horse/
Rustom's horse/White &
red mixed colour

Rakhsh-e-umr रख़्श-ए-उम्र Horse of life/Fast
passing life

Rakht-e-kesarii रख़्त-ए-केसरी Saffron apparel or
harness or chattel

Rakht-e-safar रख़्त-ए-सफ़र Things needed
on a journey/Goods of
travel/The last journey
of life/The journey
toward death

Ram-e-havaa रम-ए-हवा
Flight of breeze

Ramiida रमीदा Terrified

Rangiinii-e-husn रंगीनी-ए-हुस्न Splendour of beauty

Raqaabat रक़ाबत Rivalry
(especially in love)

Raqam रक़म Chronicle/
Put on record/Amount

Raqsaan रक़्सां Dancing

Raqs-farma रक़्स-फ़र्मा
Dancing

Rasaa रसा Reached/
Arriving/Capable/
Penetrating/Of keen
understanding/Sharp

Rasaaii रसाई Access/
Reach/Approach/
Entrance/Sharpness
(of mind)/Perspicacity/
Acuteness/ Quickness of
apprehension

Rasan रसन Rope

Rasan-o-daar रसन-ओ-दार
Death by hanging

Rashha-e-qalam रशहा-ए-
क़लम Compositions of
pen

Rashk रश्क़ Jealousy/
Envy/Malic/Spite

Rashk-e-chaman रश्क़-ए-
चमन Envy of the
garden

Rashk-e-mah रश्क़-ए- मह
Envy of the moon/
Jealous of moon/Very
beautiful

Rasman रस्मन As a matter
of tradition or custom/
Formally

Rasm-o-raah रस्म-ओ-राह
Traditions and ways

Rasuul रसूलMessenger
of God/Prophet to
who book is revealed/
Emissary/Messenger

Ratb-o-yaabis रत्ब-ओ-
याबिसWet and dry

Rau रौ Flow/Rhythm

Raulaa रौला Riot/Brawl/
Furore/Uproar

Rauunat रऊनत Pride/
Awe

Rauzaan रौज़ान Hole/
Window/Skylight

Ravaa रवा Right/Lawful/
Admissible/Current

Ravish रविश Pathway/
manners

Razaa रज़ा State of being content/Pleasure/ Consent/Assent/ Approval/Permission/ Acquiescence

Razzaaqii रज़्ज़ाक़ी Providing daily bread/ Giving the means of subsistence

Reg रेग Sand

Reg-e-ravaan रेग-ए-रवां Flying sands/Shifting sands

Rehn रैह्न Mortgage/Pledge/ Bail/Security

Resha-e-dil रेशा-ए-दिलNerve or vein or fibre or filament of heart

Reshe रेशे Veins/Roots

Reza रेज़ा Scrap/Piece/ Atom/Bit/Crumb/ Desire/Minute/A kind of cock

Rifaaqat रिफ़ाक़त Companionship/ Friendships

Rifat रिफ़त Height

Rifat-e-aflaak रिफ़अत-ए-अफ़लाकHeight of skies

Rikaab रिक़ाब Stirrup

Rindaana रिन्दानाDrunk/ Rakish/Lewd/Licentious

Rind-e-laa-ubaalii रिन्द-ए-ला-उबाली Careless drinker/The one who madly drinks

Rind-mashrab रिन्द-मशरब Drinker of drinks

Risaalon रिसालों Magazines

Rivaak रिवाक Canopy/ Roof in front of a tent/ Gallery in front of the house/Curtain stretched before the door of a house or tent

Rivaayat रिवायत Traditions

Riyaa रिया Hypocrisy/ Pretence/Dissimulation

Rizq रिज़्क़ Daily bread/ Subsistence/Livelihood/ Allowance/Sustenance/

Rizvaan रिज़वां Paradise

Roab रोआब Fear/Awe

Roshni-farosh रौशनी-फ़रोश Seller of light

Rotab रोतब Green/Verdant

Roz-e-abr रोज़-ए-अब्र Cloudy day

Roz-e-hisaab रोज़-ए-हिसाब Day of Judgement or resurrection

Roz-e-jazaa रोज़-ए-जज़ा Doomsday/Judgement day/Day of resurrection

Roz-e-panj-shamba रोज़-ए-पंज-शम्बा Thursday

Rujuua रुजूअ Recourse/ Appeal/Bias/Reference/ Turning (toward)/ Inclination/Bent/ Returning/ Leaning

Rukh-e-nikuu रुख़-ए-निकूं Beautiful face

Rukhshanda रुख़शंदा Shining/Brilliant

Rumuuz रुमूज़ Secrets

Ruqa रुक़्क़ा Note/Letter

Rusvaa रुस्वा Despondent/ Dishonoured

Rutba रुत्बा Honour

Ruu रू Basis/ Countenance/Face

Ruubaahii रूबाही Cunning/Deceit/ Trickery/Subterfuge

Ruu-ba-shaam रू-ब-शाम Face towards evening

Ruudaad रूदाद Account/ Narration/Report/ Statement

Ruuhaanii रूहानी Spiritual/Soul-releted/ Spirit-related/Hearty/ Holy/Pure/The angel

Ruuh-e-ravaan रूह-ए-रवां Moving spirit/Flowing soul/Life and soul (of party)

Ruunahiyat रूहानियत Spirituality

Ruunaahiyaan रूहानियाँ Spirits/Angels

Ruu-posh रू-पोश Hidden/
Gone into hiding/
Absconder/Wrapper/
Concealed

Ruu-poshii रू-पोशी
Disappearance/
Concealment

Ruu-siyaah रू-सियाह
Black-faced/Disgraced/
Ignominious/Sinner

Ruudaad रूदाद Report/
Statement/Minutes/
Narrative/Story

S

Sadaaqat ho to dil siinon se khinchne lagte hain vaaiz
Haqiiqat khud ko manvaa letii hai maanii nahiin jaatii
Jigar Moradabadi

Ab to saraab hii se bujhaane lage hain pyaas
Lene lage hain kaam yaqiin kaa gumaan se ham
Rajesh Reddy

Burii sarisht na badlii jagah badalne se
Chaman men aa ke bhii kaantaa gulaab ho na sakaa
Arzoo Lakhnavi

Vo taaza-dam hain nae shoabde dikhaate hue
Avaam thakne lage taaliyaan bajaate hue
Azhar Inayati

Kah rahaa hai shor-e-dariyaa se samundar kaa sukuut
Jis kaa jitnaa zarf hai utnaa hii vo khaamosh hai
Natiq Lakhnavi

Phuul the rang the lamhon kii sabaahat ham the
Aise zinda the ki jiine kii alaamat ham the
Aitbar Sajid

'Taabish' jo guzartii hii nahiin shaam kii had se
Sochen to vahii raat sahar-khez bahut hai
Abbas Tabish

Har koii dil kii hathelii pe hai sahraa rakkhe
Kis ko sairaab kare vo kise pyaasaa rakkhe
Ahmad Faraz

Vo jo sarmaaya-e-dil-o-jaan thii
Ab vahii aarzuu paraaii hai
Jaun Eliya

Bikhrii ik baar to haath aaii hai kab mauj-e-shamiim
Dil se niklii hai to kab lab pe fugaan thahrii hai
Faiz Ahmad Faiz

S

Saaadat सआदत Prosperity

Saaat साअत Time/
Moment/Hour/Clock

Saaatein साअतें Moments

Saabiqa साबिक़ा Intimacy/
Dealings

Saabit साबित Established/
Firm/Fixed/Stable/
Prove/Confirm/
Manifest/Constant/
Stationary/

Saadaat सादात
Descendents of Prophet
Muhammad and Fatima/
Respectful

Saadat सादत Blissfulness

Saada-lauh सादा-लौह
Simpleton

Saadir सादिर Flushed/
Surprised/Anxious/

Worried/Proceeding/
Issued/Passed

Saadmaanii सादमानी
Happiness

Saaebaan साएबान Canopy

Saaf-goii साफ़-
गोईFrankness of speech

Sahab-e-farm-o-zaka
साहब-ए-फ़र्म-ओ-ज़का
Men of understanding/
Pure/Pious/Chaste/
Virtuous/Just/ One
who gives the prescribed
portion of his wealth to
the poor

Saahib-e-aulaad साहिब-
ए-औलाद One who has
children

Saahib-e-dil साहिब-ए-दिल
Pious/Generous

Saahib-e-idraak साहिब-ए-इदराक Sensible person

Saahib-e-kitaab साहिब-ए-किताब One to whom God reveals a book/ Divinely ordained prophet/Author/Man of book

Saahib-e-maqduur साहिब-ए-मक़दूर Person with ability

Saail साइल Beggar/ Applicant/Petitioner/ Interrogater/Questioner

Saakin साकिन Resident/ Inhabitant/Dweller/ Stationary/Tranquil/ Calm/Peaceful/At rest

Saakin-e-dair साकिन-ए-दैर Resident of temple

Saakit साकित Immobile/ Static/Quiet/Mute/ Silent/At rest/Reticent

Saalahaa सालहा Years

Saalik सालिक Traveller/Devotee

Saane-e-qudrat साने-ए-क़ुदरत Creator of nature/God

Saaneha सानेहा Accident/ Occurrence

Saang सांग Disguise/ Mimicry/Acting a part in a play

Saanii सानी Chaff and straw mixed with grain and water as fodder/ Equal/Match/ Like

Saaqii-e-kausar साक़ी-ए-कौसर Prophet Muhammad as the steward of the heavenly spring Kausar

Saarbaan सारबां Camel driver

Saaya-e-tar साया-ए-तर Moist shadow

Saaz-baaz साज़-बाज़ Conspiracy/Intrigue

Saazgaar साज़गार Favourable

Sabaa सबा East wind/
Buying wine to sell/
Historical city of
Empress Bilkiis
contemporary of
Prophet Sulaimna

Sabaahat सबाहत Fair
complexion/Brightness
of face/Beauty/
Elegance/Comeliness/
Loveliness

Sabaat सबात Permanence/
Constancy/Stability/
Endurance/Patience/
Firmness/Durability

Sabiih सबीह Comely/
Handsome

Sabiil सबील Strategy/
Resource/Road/Path/
Way/Course/Means/
Instrument/Mode/
Method

Sabt सब्त Inscription/
Inscribed/Inspiration

Sadaa सदा Sound/Call/
Ring/Bell/Shout

Sadaa-nafas सदा-नफ़स
Breath of air

Sadaa-noshi सदा-नोशी
Absorbing sound

Sadaaqat सदाक़त Truth/
Veracity/Fidelity/
Truthfulness/Verity/
Sincerity

Sadaf सदफ़ **Oyster** shell/
Mother-of-pearl shell/
Goblet shaped like an
ouster shell

Sadiq सादिक़ Sincere

Sadqe सदक़े Alms/Offerings

Saf सफ़ Queue/Row/Line
of things or persons/
Rank/Order/Class/
Group/Prayer matof one
row of congregation

Saf-ba-saf सफ़-ब-सफ़ One
by one/In a line

Saf-e-ashjaar सफ़-ए-
अश्जार Line of trees

Saffaak सफ़्फ़ाक़ Cruel
man/Tyrant/Butcher/
Shedder of blood/
Beloved (figurative)

Safiihon सफ़ीहों Stupid persons

Safiiraan सफ़ीरां Ambassadors

Safiiron सफ़ीरों Ambassadors

Sahaab सहाब Cloud

Sahaafii सहाफ़ी Journalist

Sahba सहबा Wine, especially red

Sahar-e-kaazib सहर-ए-क़ाज़िब Time just before daybreak/False dawn

Sahar-gaahii सहर-ग़ाही Awakening/Sunrise/Morning/Food taken early morning for the purpose of fasting

Sahar-khez सहर-ख़ेज़ Early riser

Saharii सहरी Of or relating to the dawn/Of morning

Sahiifa सहीफ़ा Leaf/Page/Magazine/Book/Volume/Periodical/Book revealed to a divinely ordained prophet/Letter/Charter

Sahiifa-e-jaan सहीफ़ा-ए-जान Revelation of life

Sahl-angaarii सहल-अंगारी Taking easy/Carelessness

Sahl-talab सहल-तलब Easy-going

Sahn सहन Courtyard

Sahraa सहरा Desert/Wilderness/Plain

Sahraa-gard सहरा-गर्द Desert wanderer

Sahuulat सहूलत Ease/Facility

Sahv सह्व Error/Mistake/Negligence

Saii सई Effort/Endeavour/Advance payment

Saii-e-karam सई-ए-करम Kind effort

Saii-e-musalsal Continuous effort

Sail सैल Flood

Sail-e-ashk सैल-ए-अश्क़ Flood of tears

Saili सैली Slap

Sairaab सैराब Fertile/ Flourishing/Bloomiong/ Moist/Replete/Well-watered

Sair-e-maqaamaat-e-dil-fareb सैर-ए-मक़ामात-ए-दिल-फ़रेब Outings to heart-ravishing places

Sakhaavat सख़ावत Generosity

Sakhii सख़ी Generous/ Donor/Liberal/ Bountiful/A generous or bountiful person

Sakht-jaan सख़्त-जां Callous

Sakht-jaanii सख़्त-जानी Hard life

Sakit साकित Immobile/ Static/Mute/Silent/ Reticent

Salaa-e-aam सला-ए-आम Open invitation to all

Salaamat सलामत Peace/ Safety/State of being secure from danger or harm/Sacurely/Safely/ Safe

Salaasil सलासिल Chains/ Shackles

Saliib सलीब Crucifix/ Gallows/Torture/ Agony/Brave/ Courageous/Hard/ Firm/

Saltanat-e-aalam सल्तनत-ए-आलम Kingdom of the world

Samaa समा Sky/Heaven/ Time

Samaaat समाअत Hearing power/ Hearing/Sese of hearing/Attention/ Listening(of a lawsuit)

Samaaii समाई Capacity/ Capability/ Patience

Samaane समाने Go or fit into/Take up room/Fill or occupy space/To be contained in

Saman समन Jasmine

Saman-khaanon समन-ख़ानों Idol houses/Temples

Samar समर Fruit

Samarvar समरवर Laden with fruit

Samo समो High/Tall/Elevated

Sanaa-khvaan सना-ख़्वां Praise reciter/One who praises

Sanad सनद Charter/Diploma/Patent

Sanam-khaanon सनम-ख़ानों Idol houses/Temples

Sang-e-giraan संग-ए-गिरां Heavy stone

Sang-e-khaaraa संग-ए-ख़रा Hard stone/Flint

Sang-zan संग-ज़न Stone pelter/One who treats cruelly/Stone-peddler/Dubious weighing scale/A light pair of scales

Sanobar सनोबर Pine tree

Sapedii सपेदी Grey hair

Sar सर On/At

Saraab सराब Mirage

Saraapaa सरापा Human figure from head to foot

Sar-afraaz सर-अफ़्राज़ Promoted/Exalted

Sar-ba-sar सर-ब-सर Entirely/Whole/Completely

Sar-ba-kaf सर-ब-कफ़ One who is willing to die/Bravery

Sar-chashma-e-baqaa सर-चश्म-ए-बक़्क़ा Source of elixir of immortality

Sardaadgaan सरदादगां Chiefs

Sard-mehrii सर्द-मैहरी
Indifference/Cold
attitude/Negligence/
Ingratitude

Sar-e-qirtaas सर-ए-क़िर्तास
On the face of a page

Sar-e-silsila सर-ए-
सिलसिला Beginning of
continuum

Sarf सर्फ़ Use/Busy/
Expenditure/
Extravaganza/Expense/
Unadulterated/Pure/
Unmixed/Neat

Sarfaraaz सर्फ़राज़
Eminent/Exalted/
Distinguished

Sarf-e-tapish सर्फ़-ए-तपिश
Use of heat

Sargarm सरगर्म Busy/
Active

*Sargashta-e-khumaar-
e-russum-e-qayyud*
सरगश्ता-ए-खुमार-
ए-रुस्सुम-ए-क़य्युद
Bewildered by
intoxication of

restrictions and
traditional traditions

Sar-giraan सर-गिरां
Restless/Anxious

Sargoshii सरग़ोशी
Whisper/Gossip/
Speaking in a low voice

Sarguzisht सरगुज़िश्त
Biography

Sariir-e-khaama सरीर-ए-
ख़ामा Scratching sound
made by the pen

Sarisht सरिश्त
Temperament

Sar-kashii सर-कशी
Rebellion

Sar-kashiida सर-कशीदा
Inspired from head

Sarmastii सरमस्ती
Intoxication

Sarmaaya सरमाया Capital/
Principal amount/
Wealth/Financial means

Sar-naame सर-नामे Letter-
heads

Sar-niguun सर-निगूं
Vanquished

Sarosh सरोश Angel/ Heavenly voice/Supreme intellect

Sarpat सर्पट Gallop/Run with fast speed/Quickly

Sarsabz सरसब्ज़ Fertile/ Fruitful/Productive/ Prosperous/Flourishing/ Verdant

Sarsarii सरसरी Cursorily/ Casually/Lacking in attention

Sarshaar सरशारBrimming with joy/Intoxicated/ Esctasy

Sarshaarii सरशारी Intoxication

Sarshaarii-e-fazaa सरशारी-ए-फ़ज़ा Intoxication of environment or ambience

Sarv सर्व Cypress

Sarv-qaamat सर्व-क़ामत Tall height

Sarzad सर्ज़द To be committed/Occurred/ Happened

Sataaish सताइश Accolade/ Praise/Appreciation/ Eulogy/Benediction

Sataaish-gar सताइश-गर One who praises/ appreciates

Sath-e-zehen-e-aalam सथ-ए-ज़हन-ए-आलम Level of mind of the world

Sauubaton सौबतों Difficulties

Sauda सौदा Frenzy/Madness/ Goods/Trade/Purchase

Saudaa-garii सौदा-गरी Melancholia/Trade

Saudaaii सौदाई Lovesick/ Melancholic/Crazy/Insane

Saum-o-salaat सौम-ए-सलात Fast and prayer

Sauudii-tartiib सऊदी-तरतीब Ascending order

Savaab सवाब Reward/ Recompense/Requital/ Reward esp of obedience to God/Meritorious act/ The reward of virtue in a future state

Savaab-e-sidq-o-vafaa सवाब-ए-सिद़क़-ओ-वफ़ा Grace of truth and constancy

Savaabit सवाबित The fixed stars/Stars

Savaab-e-taaat-o-zohd सवाब-ए-तआत-ओ-ज़ोहद Blessings by obedience and devoutness

Savaad सवाद A large number/Ability(to read and write)/Anything written/Manuscript/Draft/Black colour or ink

Savaad-e-shahr सवाद-ए-शहर Environs of the city

Sayyaar सय्यार Moving/Wanderer

Sayyaare सय्यारे Planets

Sayyargaan सय्यारगां Planets

Sayyaaron सय्यारों Wanderers/Travellers/Tourists

Sazaavaar सज़ावार Deserving of punishment/Punishable

Sazaa-yab सज़ा-यब Awarded with punishment/Penalized or sentenced person

Seb-e-gabgab सेब-ए-गबगब Dimple in chin

Sehn सेहन Courtyard

Shab-khuun शब्-ख़ून Night attack

Shaadaab शादाब Verdant/Blooming green

Shaadaabii शादाबी Greenery

Shaadmaan शादमां Happy

Shaahid शाहिद Eye witness

Shaakii शाक़ी One who complains

Shaam-e-alam शाम-ए-अलम Evening of sorrow

Shaam-e-gariibaan शाम-ए-गरीबां Evening full of calamities/Night of mourners/Mourning night observed by Shias in Muharram

Shaam-e-shakebaaii शाम-ए-शकेबाई Evening of patience

Shaan-e-kariimii शान-ए-क़रीमी Majesty of God's kindness

Shaana शाना Adult/Elder/Decent/Smart/Elegant/Glory/Comb/Shoulder

Shaayaan शायान Proper/Fit/Suitable/Worthy

Shabaab-e-rafta शबाब-ए-रफ़्ताBygone beauty

Shab-e-vaslat शब्-ए-वसलतNight of sexual union

Shabaahaten शबाहतें Resemblance (plural)/Look-alike

Shab-e-baraat शब्-ए-बरात 15th night of Islamic month of shaabaan (month before Ramadan)

Shab-e-mahtaab शब्-ए-महताब Moonlit night

Shab-e-taar शब्-ए-तार Dark night

Shab-gaziida शब्-ग़ज़ीदा Injured or hurt by night

Shabiih शबीह Image/Portrait/Picture/Resemblance

Shabistaan शबिस्तां Bed chamber/Covered part of a mosque

Shab-rang शब्-रंग Dark coloured

Shab-taab शब्-ताब Bright night

Shadeed शदीद Intense

Shafaaf शफ़ाफ़ Clear/Limpid/Transparent/Bright/Open to public scrutiny/Morally correct

Shafaq शफ़क़ Evening twilight

Shafqat शफ़क़त Affectionate kindness/Clemency

Shagaf शग़ाफ़ Inclination/Interest/Liking/Fondness/Enthusiasm

Shagl शग़्ल Hobby

Shagufta शगुफ़्ता
Refreshed/Flourishing/
Bloomed/Cheerful/
Happy

Shaguftagii शगुफ़्तगी
Cheerfulness/Delight/
Pleasure

Shaguufa शगूफ़ा Bud

Shahaadat शहादत
Witness/Evidence/
Testimony/Martyrdom

Shahar-aaraa शहर-
आरा Embellishing/
Decorating city

Shahbaaz शाहबाज़ Brave
man/Handsome young
man/Falcon

Shahar-e-fusuun शहर-
ए-फ़ुसूँ Magical or
spellbinding city

Shah-e-mardaan शाह-ए-
मर्दा King of heroes/
Hazrat Ali

Shah-nishaan-e-dil शाह-
निशाँ-ए-दिल Heart's
throne

Shahr-aaraa शहर-
आरा Embellishing or
decorating city

Shahr-e-badar शहर-ए-बदर
Banish/Exile

Shahr-e-jaan शहर-ए-जां
City of life/Self/Body

Shahr-e-khamoshaan
शहर-ए-खामोशां Cemetry

Shah-nashiin शाह-नशीं
Throne

Shahriyat शहरियत
Citizenship

Shahvat शहवत Lust/
Sensuality/Sexual urge

Shah-zor शह-ज़ोर
Powerful

Shaidaa शइदा Infatuation/
Enamored/Deeply in
love/Deep ardour

Shajar शजर Tree

Shakal-e-shabaahat
शकल-ए-शबाहत Visage
and resemblance

Shakebaaii शकेबाई
Patience/Tolerance/
Endurance

Shama-e-bazm शमअ-ए-बज़्म Lamp of assembly

Shamiim शमीम Fragrance/Perfume/Aroma/Smell/Odour

Shams शम्स Sun

Shanaas शनास Knowing/Acquainted with/Intelligence/Knowledge

Shanaasaa शनासा Familiar

Shanaasaaii शनासाई Acquaintance/Knowledge/The state of being acquainted

Shanaasii शनासी Awareness/The act of knowing/The act of identifying

Shanaavar शनावर Swimmer

Sharaab-e-arsh शराब-ए-अर्श Celestial wine

Sharaab-e-naab शराब-ए-नाब Red wine

Sharaab-e-tahuur शराब-ए-तहूर Holy wine/Pure drinks mentioned in the Quran which do not contain intoxicants

Sharaf शरफ़ To be or become exalted

Sharar शरर Spark/Flash

Sharh शर्ह Interpretation/Explanation/Exposition/Meaning

Sharhen शर्हें Explanations/Interpretations

Sharminda-e-ehsaan शर्मिंदा-ए-एहसान Beholden to/Under obligation to

Sharmsaar शर्मसार Ashamed/Regretting

Sharq शर्क़ Rising/East

Sharraah शर्राह Interpreter

Shart-e-fan शर्त-ए-फ़न Condition for success

Shashdar शश्दर Perplexed/Astonished/Confounded

Shash-jihaat शश-जिहात Six facets/Hexagon/All the six sides/All sides of the universe

Shauq शौक़ Eagerness/
Fondness/Zeal/Ardour/
Desire/Hobby/Passion/
Longing/Pleasure

Shauq-e-fuzuul शौक़-ए-
फ़ुज़ूल Useless pursuit

Shauq-e-vaalihaana शौक़-
ए-वालिहाना Desperate
love

Shaayaan शायां Fit (for)/
Suitable/Desirable

Shefta शेफ़्ता Enamoured
with love

Sheva शेवा Manner/Habit/
Way/Method

Shevan शेवन Lamentation/
Grief/Mourning

Sheva-e-guftaar शेवा-ए-
गुफ़्तार Style of speech

Shiaar शिआर Method/
Custom/Countersign

Shiaarii शिआरी
Conditioned to

Shiddat शिद्दत Force/
Severity/Intensity

Shifaa शिफ़ा Healing/

Cure/Recovery/
Recovery(from illness)/
Convalescence/
Medicine/Remedy

Shikaar-e-murda शिकार-
ए-मुर्दा Hunt of the dead

Shikam शिकम Stomach

Shikam-ser शिकम-सेर Full
stomach

Shiir शीर Milk

Shiir-o-shakkar शीर-ओ-
शक्कर Close intimacy/
Hand in glove/Very
close and intimate

Shiiraaza शीराज़ा Binding
(of book)/Arrangement/
Management/Ends of
the stitching of a book

Shiisha-e-saaat शीशा-ए-
साअतHourglass

Shirk शिर्क Polytheism

Shirkat शिर्कत
Participation/
Partnership/Company

Shitaab शिताब Quick/
Speed/Haste

Shitaabii शिताबी
Quickness/Haste/Speed/
Swiftness/Uneasiness/
Anxiety/Perturbation

Shoala-zaar शोअला-ज़ार
Field of embers/Light/
Flames

Shoabadagar शोअबदागर
Illusionist

Shoabadakaaron
शोअबदाकारों Jugglers

Shoabde शोअब्दे Magic/
Tricks

Shohra शोहरा Fame/
Reknown/Reputation/
Acknowledgement

Shohra-e-aafaaq शोहरा-ए-
आफ़ाक़ Of worldwide
fame

Shor-e-talaatum शोर-ए-
तलातुम Noise of storm

Shoriida-sar शोरीदा-
सर Mad/Rebellious/
Demented/Desperate/
Dejected/Melancholy/
Tempestuous/
Desperately (in love)

Shoriidgii शोरीदग़ी
Confusion/Tumult/
Rebellion/Craziness/
Passion

Shorish शोरीश Tumult

Shubh शुब्ह Doubt

Shuhra शुहरा Fame

Shuhuud शुहूद Anything
that is apparent and can
be seen/Friday/Day of
resurrection/Witnesses

Shumaar शुमार Countig/
Numbering/Number/
Account

Shuniidan शुनीदां Listening

Shuruua शुरूअ Beginning

Shusta शुस्ता Pure/
Cleaned/Washed/
Chaste/Pure (language)/
Cultivated

Shusta-mizaaj शुस्ता-
मिज़ाज Cultivated
temperament

Shuuur शुऊर
Consciousness/Wisdom

Sidq-o-safaa सिद्क़-ओ-सफ़ा Truth and purity

Sifaal सिफ़ाल Earthenware/ Earth/Soil/Clay/Cover/ Shell (esp decorated with flowery design)

Sifat सिफ़त Attribute/ Quality/Trait/ Characteristic/Fetire/ Epithet/Praise

Sifaat सिफ़ात Qualities

Siflaa सिफ़्ला Sordid/Vile/ Base/Ignoble/Low/ Mean

Siim सीम Silver

Siim-tan सीम –तन Silver- bodied/Fair

Siirat सीरत Quality/ Nature/Disposition/ Character

Sila सिला Reward/Gift/ Present

Sin सिन Age

Sinaan सिनां Spears/ Swords/Tips of arrows

Sipar सिपर Shield/Bold/ Undaunted/Secure/ Assistant

Sitaan सितां Place where anything dwells

Sitam-zariif सितम-ज़रीफ़ One who practices tyranny in a subtle and dextrous way

Sitaara-e-saharii सितारा- ए-सहरी Morning star

Sivaa सिवा But/Over and above/Except/Besides

Siyaah-chashmagii सियाह-चश्मगी Dark eyes

Siyaam सियाम Ramzan

Siyah-faam सियाह-फ़ाम Dark comlexion

Soam सोअम Conceit/ Arrogance

Sog सोग Grief/ Lamentations/Sorrow/ Mourning

Sogvaar सोगवर Sad/ Grieved/Sorrowful

Sogvaaron सोगवारों
Mourners

Sohbatein सोहबतें
Company

Sokhta सोख़्ता Burnt/ Grieved/Dejected/ Lovesick/A piece of burning wood/Blotting paper/Slow match/Flint

Soz सोज़ Burning/Sorrow/ Heart-burning

Soz-e-jaan-gudaaz सोज़-ए-जान-गुदाज़ Passion of delicate life

Soz-e-taaza सोज़-ए-ताज़ा New passion or love

Subh-dam सुबह-दम Early morning/Dawn

Subh-e-azal सुबह-ए-अज़ल Beginning of eternity/ Time when existence came to being/Morning of eternity

Subh-e-kaazib सुबह-ए-काज़िब False morning/ Time just before daybreak

Subh-gaahii सुबह-ग़ाही Relating to dawn or morning

Subha सुबहा Rosary

Subuk सुबुक Light

Subuk-ruuh सुबुक़-रूह Cheerful/Merry/Jovial

Subuu सुबू Goblet/Jar/ Pitcher/Glass/Cup

Sukhan सुख़न Talk/ Speech/Dialogue/ Converse/News/ Discourse/Poetry

Sukhan-e-sakht सुख़न-ए-सख़्त Harsh or difficult words

Sukhan-fahmii सुख़न-फ़हमी Understanding poetry

Sukhan-haa-e-guftanii सुख़न-हा-ए-गुफ़्तानी Quotable words

Sukhan-varii सुख़न-वरी Eloquence/Poetry/The art of composing poetry

Sukr सुक्र To be or become intoxicated/ Intoxicant or alcoholic drink/Intoxication/ Drunkenness

Sukuut सुकूत Silence/ Quietness/Peace

Sulh-e-kul सुलह-ए-कुल Perfect reconciliation/ Definitive treaty/Peace-loving/Peace with all

Sukuut-e-shab सुकूत-ए-शब् Silence of the night

Sulataanii-e-jambuur सुलतानी-ए-जमहूर Rule of democracy

Sumbul सुम्बुल Hyacinth

Summa-aahaa सुम्मा-आहा Act of sighing in pain

Supurd-e-naar-e-ishq सुपुर्द-ए-नार-ए-इश्क़ Surrender to the fire of love

Surat-nigaaraan सूरत-निगारां Painters/Artists

Surkh सुर्ख Red

Surkh-ruu सुर्ख-रू Honoured/Exonerated/ Successful/Unashamed

Surkh-ruuii सुर्ख-रूई Success

Suruur सुरूर Pleasure/Joy/ Enjoyment/Cheerfulness

Sust-al-vajuud सुस्त-अल-वजूद Lazy bones

Sutuun सुतूं Pillar

Suu सू Directions

Suu-e-matluub सू-ए-मतलूब Towards what is sought

Suud सूद Profit/Interest/ Gain

Suurat-e-bayaan सूरत-ए-बयां Style or way or mannerof narrative

Suurat-e-diivaar सूरत-ए-दीवार Face of wall

Suurat-e-gufl-e-abjad सूरत-ए-गुफ़्ल-ए-अबजद A kind of coded lock/A lock with numbers/A puzzle

T

Khvaab dekhaa thaa mohabbat kaa mohabbat kii qasam
Phir isii khvaab kii taabiir men masruuf thaa main
Khalid Malik Sahil

Tadbiir mere ishq kii kyaa faaeda tabiib
Ab jaan hii ke saath ye aazaar jaaegaa
Meer Taqi Meer

Unhen to sitam kaa mazaa pad gayaa hai
Kahaan kaa tajaahul kahaan kaa tagaaful
Bekhud Dehlvi

Uljhaa hai magar zulf men taqriir kaa lachhaa
Suljhii huii ham ne na sunii baat tumhaarii
Muneer Shikohabadi

Yaad men khvaab men tasavvur men
Aa ki aane ke hain hazaar tariiq
Bayan Meeruthi

Har shab-e-gam kii sahar ho ye zaruurii hai magar
Sab kii taabinda sahar ho ye zaruurii to nahiin
Habeeb Hashmi

Tafriiq husn-o-ishq ke andaaz men na ho
Lafzon men farq ho magar aavaaz men na ho
Manzar Lakhnavi

Ik husn-e-be-misaal kii tamsiil ke liye
Parchhaaiyon pe rang giraataa rahaa huun main
Jaun Eliya

Tasadduq is karam ke main kabhii tanhaa nahiin rahtaa
Ki jis din tum nahiin aate tumhaarii yaad aatii hai
Jaleel Manikpuri

Sabz hotii hii nahiin ye sarzamiin
Tukhm-e-khvaahish dil men tuu botaa hai kyaa
Meer Taqi Meer

T

Taaam तआम Meals/
Victuals

Taaaqub तआक़ुब Pursuit/
Chase/Following

Taaat ताअत Act
of devotion/
Obsequiousness/
Obedience/Submission

Taaavun तआवुन
Assistance/
Cooperation/Mutual
aid/The effect of
increasing the potency or
effectiveness of a drug or
treatment

Taa-ba-kujaa ता-बा-कुजा Up
to where, whither/How
far/How long/Till when

Taa-dum-e-marg ता-दम-ए-
मर्ग Till the time of death

Taab ताब Endurance/
Bright/Tolerance/
Warmth/Heat

Taabaan ताबां Bright/
Shining

Taa-ba-adab ता-ब-अदब
Up to eternity

Taabaanii ताबानी
Brightness

Taa-ba-qadam ता-ब-क़दम
Up to step

Taab-e-hijraan ताब-ए-
हिज्राँ Tolerance for
separation

Taabiir ताबीर
Interpretation of dream

Taabinda ताबिंदा Bright/
Luminous/Sparkling/
Shining

Taabish ताबिश Splendour

Taahid ताहिद Protect

Taaib ताइब Repentant/
Abstinent/Penitent

Taaiid ताइद
Encouragement/
Ratification/Aid/Help/
Support/Advocacy/
Confirmation/
Corroboration/
Justification

Taaiid-e-haq ताइद-ए-हक़
Confirmation of truth

Taajvarii ताजवारी
Kingship

Taakhiir ताख़ीर Delay/
Retardation/Lateness/
Procastination

Taakiid ताक़ीद Stress/
Emphasis/Pressure/
Admonition/Injunction/
Accent

Taala ताला Fortune

Taala-e-bedaar ताला-ए-
बेदार Awakened fortune

Taalib तालिब Candidate

Taam ताम Food/Victuals

Taa-maqduur ता-मक़दूर
To the best of one's
ability

Taamiir तामीर Building/
Construction/Repair/
Act of construction/
Erection of edifices

Taaq ताक़ Niche/Unique

Taaq-e-har-manzar ताक़-
ए-हर-मंज़र Niche of
every view/Scene

Taaqon ताक़ों Niches/
Holes in wall

Taar तार Darkness/
Tatters

Taaraaj ताराज Plunder/
Devastation/
Destruction/Ruin

Taasii तासी Cover/
Make-up/Obedience/
Submission/Observance

Taasiir तासीर
Effectiveness/Efficact/
Influence/Impression/
Effect/The making of an
impression

Taassuf तअस्सुफ़ Regret/ Remorse/Contrition/ Compunction/ Repentance/Pity/Grief/ Sorrow/ Commiseration

Taassur तासूर Impression/ Affect/Feeling

Taassuub तासूब Prejudice against or for

Taauus ताऊस Peacock

Taayyun तअय्युन Determining/ Fixing/Assigning/ Appointment/ Establishment

Taaza-dam ताज़ा-दम Refreshed

Taaziiren ताज़ीरें Articles of law

Taaziir ताज़ीर Punishment

Taaziim ताज़ीम Respect/ Reverence/Honour/ Oberisance/Adoration

Tabaa तबा Nature/ Temperament/Print

Tabaah-kun तबाह-कुन Devastating

Tabaq तबक़ Large tray or dish/Region/World

Tabassum तबस्सुम Smile

Tabeeb तबीब Doctor

Tab-e-khud-aaraa तब-ए-ख़ुद-आरा Self-exhibiting nature

Tab-e-ravaan तब-ए-रवां Smooth nature/Mellow disposition

Tabiiii तबीई Natural

Tabsire तबसिरे Reviews

Tadaave तदावे Offering

Tadbeer तदबीर Plan

Tadriis तदरीस Teaching/ Instruction/Education

Tafaavut तफ़ावुत Difference/Disparity/ Diversity/Distance/ Discordance/ Distinction/Interval/ Dissimilar/Being far apart

Tafraqa तफ़रक़ा Conflict/ Discord

Tafriiq तफ़रीक़

Separation/Division/
Departure/Subtraction/
Discrimination/
Separating/Subtraction/
Discrimination/
Misunderstanding

Tafsiir तफ़सीर

Explanation

Tagaaful तग़ाफ़ुल

Negligence/Feigned
negligence/Indifference/
Inattention/Laxity/
Laziness

Tagaaful-saraa तग़ाफ़ुल-
सरा Ignorant

Tagayyur तग़य्युर

Alteration/Change/
Difference/
Diversity/Mutation/
Discrepancy

Tagiyaani तग़ियानी Flood/
Inundation

Tahaffuz तहफ़्फ़ुज़

Security/Protection/
Safeguarding/
Preservation/
Conservation

Tahammul तहम्मुल

Patience/Endurance/
Toleration/Forbearance/
Liberality

Tahayya तहय्या

Determination/
Provision/Putting in
order/Resolve

Tahayya-e-tuufaan
तहय्या-ए-तूफ़ान

Determination for
storm

Tahayyur तहय्युर

Amazement/
Astonishment/Wonder/
Being astonished or
confounded

Tah-e-daruun
तह-ए-दरूं

Bottom of inside

Tahii-dast तही-दस्त

Impoverished hands

Tahliil तहलील The act of
making lawful/Finishing
prayer and offering
salutation after finishing/
Praising God/

***Tahniyat* तहनियत** Good news/Congratulations/Good wishes/Wishing one joy and prosperity

***Tahqiiq* तहक़ीक़** Research

***Tahriik* तहरीक़** Putting in motion/Proposal/Suggestion/Temptation/Movement

***Tahriir* तहरीर** Writing/Composition/Document

***Tahsiin* तहसीन** Acclamation/Appreciation

***Tahuur* तहूर** Pure/Clean/Purifying/Cleansing/Water with which one cleanses or purifies

***Taiin* तईं** Till (**तक** in Hindi)

***Tajaahul* तजाहुल** Apathy/Indifference/Pretended ignorance/Overlooking

***Tajallii* तजल्ली** Splendour/Brightness/Brilliance/Refulgence/Lustre

***Tajassus* तजस्सुस** Curiosity/Inquisitiveness/Search/Enquiry/Investigating/Exploring

***Tajdiid* तज्दीद** Renewal/Renovation/Revival

***Taj-e-sar* ताज-ए-सर** Crowned head

***Tajviiz* तजवीज़** Proposal/Scheme/Plan/View/Opinion/Judgement/Permiting/Allowing/Approving

***Takaan* तकां** Weariness/Fatigue/Tiredness/Motion/Movement/Jolt/Jerk/Bump

***Takabbur* तकब्बुर** Pride/Arrogance/Haughtiness/Insolence/Egotism/Conceit

***Takallum* तकल्लुम** Conversation

***Takbiir* तकबीर** Saying God is great/Words said before the Islamic prayer begins

***Takhayyul* तख़य्युल** Imagination/Fancy/Idea/Thought/Imagery

Takhliiq तख़्लीक़ Creation/
Compilation/Invention

Takhliiq-kaar तख़लीक़-
कार Creator

Takhliya तख़्लिया Privacy/
Solitude

Takhmiine तख़मीने
Estimates

Takiya तकिया Reliance/
Trust/Prop/Support/
Anything upon which
one leans/Pillow/
Bolster

Takmiil तक़मील
Completion/
Consummation/
Flawlessness/
Effectuation/Execution/
Integration

Takmiil-e-safar तक़मील-
ए-सफ़र Completion of
journey

Takraar तक़रार Argument/
Altercation/Dispute/
Repetition

Talaafii तलाफ़ी
Recompense/Redress/
Making amends/
Compensation/
Reparation

Talab तलब Demand

Talaatum तलातुम Storm/
Tumult/Ebb and flow/
Choppiness/Roughness
of sea/Buffeting of
waves

Talkh तल्ख
Bitter/Pungent/
Unpleasant/Rancorous/
Malicious/Acrimonious

Talkh-kaamii तल्ख-कामी
Bitterness

Talkh-navaaii
तल्ख-नवाई
Saying bitter things/
Unpleasant talk

Talmiih तलमीह Allusion/
Reference to some past
event or story in one's
writing

Talqiin तल्क़ीन
Instruction

Tamaa तमअ Greed/
Avarice/Covetousness

Tamaasha-gaah-e-soz-e-taaza तमाशा-गाह-ए-सोज़-ए-ताज़ा Theatre of new passion or burning in love

Tamaazat तमाज़त Intense heat

Tamhiid तम्हीद Excuse/Preamble/Preface/Introduction/Arrangement/Adjustment

Tamkanat तमकनत Dignity/Majesty

Tamsiil तमसील Likening

Tanaab तनाब Tent-rope

Tanaazur तनाज़ुर Perspective/Scenario/Range of vision

Tanaafur तनाफ़ुर Aversion/Disgust/Utter dislike

Tanak तनक Taunt/Jeer/Reproach/Sneer

Tan-e-uryaan तन-ए-उर्यां Naked body

Tang-daamaanii तंग-दामानी Narrowness

Tanqiid तंक़ीद Criticism/Fault-finding/Judgement

Tanuur तनूर Oven

Tanuur-e-vaqt तनूर-ए-वक़्त Oven of time

Tanviir तन्वीर Illumination

Tanz तंज़ Satire/Sarcasm/Sneer

Tapaak तपाक Cordiality/Warmth

Tap-e-ishq तप-ए-इश्क़ Burning in love

Tap-e-saudaa तप-ए-सौदा Heat of madness/frenzy

Tapish तपिश Heat/Warmth/Distress/Uneasiness/Agitation

Taqaazaa तक़ाज़ा Demand/Urge/Pressing settlement/Demanding

Taqdiim तक़दीम Division

Tagdiir-e-umam तक़दीर-ए-उमम Destiny of followers

Taqliid तक़्लीद
Conformity/Being a conformist/To follow old ways and traditions/Imitation/Forgery/Counterfeiting/Mimicry/Investiture

Taqriib तक़रीब Ceremonial occasion/Function/Commemoration/Bringing near

Taqriib-e-mulaqat तक़रीब-ए-मुलाक़ात Time for meeting

Taqreer तक़रीर Speech

Taqsiim तक़सीम Distribute/Division/Partition

Taqsiim-e-aab-o-gil तक़सीम-ए-आब-ओ-गिल Division of water and clay (soil)/The constitution of man/Human body/The elements that make up the universe/

Base/Foundation/Temperament/Nature

Tarab तरब Cheerfulness/Joy/Happiness/Mirth/Merriment/Hilarity/Violin strings

Tarab-zaaron तरब-ज़ारों Music places

Tarah-daar तरह-दार Elegant/Graceful/Beautiful/Handsome

Tarannum तरन्नुम Singing/Sweet recitation/Way of singing/Words uttered in a musical tone

Tarashshoh तरश्शोह Drizzle/Sprinkling

Tardiid तर्दीद Repudiation/Rebuttal/Denial/Rejection/Contradiction

Targiib तर्गीब Temptation/Allurement/Incitement/Stimulation/Inducement/Instigation/Persuasion

Tariiq-e-kohkan तरीक़-ए-कोहकन The way of digging a mountain

Tarjumaan तर्जुमां
Interpretations/
Translations/
Spokesperson

Tarjumaan-e-shauq
तर्जुमां-ए-शौक़
Interpreters of love

Tark-e-shakebaaii तर्क-
ए-शकेबाई Renouncing
of patience/Renouncing
tolerance/Long-suffering

Tarrar तर्रार Sharp/
Eloquent

Tartiib तर्तीब
Arrangement/Order

Tarz तर्ज़ Mode/Form/
Style/Manner

Tarz-e-fugaan तर्ज़-ए-फुगां
Style of crying

Tasaadum तसादुम
Collision/Clash/
Conflict/Quarrel/
Encounter

Tasadduq तसद्दुक़
Sacrifice/Alms/Charity/
Oblation

Tasalsul तसलसुल
Succession/Series/
Sequence/Connecting
like a chain/Continuous/
Continuation/

Tasarruf तसर्रुफ़
Possession/Use/
Occupancy/
Extravagance/Change/
Management/Disposal/
Expenditure/Dominion/
Utilisation

Tasarruf-e-ishq तसर्रुफ़-ए-
इश्क़ Consummation or
consumption of
love

Tasavvur तसव्वुर
Imagination/
Contemplation

Tasavvuf तसव्वुफ़
Spirituality/Islamic
mysticism/Devotion/
Abstinence from worldly
pleasures/Sufism

Tasbiih तस्बीह
Rosary

Tasdiiq तस्दीक़ Attesting/ Verifying/Proving true/Athenticating/ Attestation/ Authentication/ Affirmation/ Verification/ Confirmation

Tashaddud तशद्दुद Violence/Aggression

Tashaffii तशफ़्फ़ी Consolation/ Satisfaction/Calmness

Tashbiib तशबीब Introduction to ode/ Introductory couplet of Qasida

Tashbiih तशबीह Simili/ Similitude/Comparison

Tashdiid तश्दीद Contravention

Tashhiir तश्हीर Publicity/ Infamy/Disgrace/ Proclaiming/Public exposure

Tashviish तशवीश Grief/ Anxiety/Concern/

Confusion/Worry/ Apprehension/ Perplexity

Taskhiir तश्क़ीर Capturing/Conquering/ Subjugating/ Captivating/Subjugation of spirits

Taskiin तस्कीन Consolation/Comfort/ Pacifying/Soothing

Taskiin-e-mahzuun-e-dil तस्कीन-ए-महज़ून-ए-दिल Satisfaction of melancholic heart

Tasliim तस्लीम Obeisance/ Homage/Conceding/ Acknowledging/Saluting respectfully/Delivering/ Consigning/Committing to the care of/Surrender

Tauf-e-haram तौफ़-ए-हरम Circuambulation of Kaaba

Taufiiq तौफ़ीक़ God's grace/Divine guidance/ Ability/Help

Tauhiid तोहीद Monotheism/Declaring God to be one

Tauqiir तौक़ीर Respect/ Honour/Veneration/ Reverence

Tausan तौसन Horse/ Uncontrolled horse/ Steed/War horse/Young unbroken horse

Tausiif तौसीफ़ Praise/ Admiration/Accolade/ Eulogy/Commendation

Tavaaf तवाफ़ Circling around the Kabah seven times/Going round/ Moving in circles/ Circulate/Turning

Tavaazo तवाज़ो Humility/ Civility/Politeness/ Hospitality/Courteous welcome

Tavahhum तवहहुम Superstition

Tavakkul तवक्कुल Trust in God/Faith

Tavajjo तवज्जो Attention/ Favour/Regard/ Inclination

Tavangar तवंगर Rich/ Powerful

Tavaqqo तवक्क़ो Expectation/Hope/ Desire/Wish

Tavaqquf तवक्क़ुफ़ Delay/ Hesitation/Pause

Taviil तवील Long

Tavaazun तवाज़ुन Equilibrium/ Balance/Poise/ Counterbalance

Tayammum तयम्मुम Purifying oneself before prayers with water or dust where water is not available

Tazaad-e-jazbaat तज़ाद-ए-जज़्बात Contradiction of emotions

Tazaamat तज़ामत Intense heat

Tazabzub तज़बजुब Dilemma

Taziin तज़ीन Embellishment/ Decoration

Taziin-e-aalam तज़ीन-ए-आलम Embellishment of the world

Tazliil तज़लील Humiliation/ Degradation

Tazkira तज़्किरा Description/Biography/ Memoir/Discussion/ Remembrance/ Narration

Tehqeeq तैहक़ीक़ Queries

Tesha तेशा Axe/Hatchet/ Chisel

Tez-rau तेज़-रौ Fast- moving/Fast speed/ Swift

Thaan थान Stall for horse or cattle/Place to stay

Thath थथ Mob

Tibaa तिबअ Nature/ Habit

Tifl तिफ़्ल Male child

Tiflaana तिफ़्लाना Childish/Childlike

Tiflii तिफ़्ली Childhood/ Infancy

Tihii तिही Empty/Vacant/ Void

Tiinat तीनत Disposition/ Temperament

Tiira तीरा Dark

Tiira-bakht तीरा-बख़्त Unfortunate/Unlucky

Tiira-o-taar तीरा-ओ-तार Darkness

Tiira-shab तीरा-शब् Dark night

Tiirgii तीरगी Darkness/ Gloom

Tiirgii-dushman तीरगी- दुश्मन Optimistic/ Hopeful/Positive

Timsaal तिमसालLikeness/ Portrait/Picture/Image/ Figure/Resemblance

Tishna तिश्ना Thirsty/ Longing/Pining for/ Insatiable

Tishna-kaam तिश्ना-काम Deprived/ Thirsty/Unlucky/ Hopeless/Unfortunate/ Unsuccessfully

Tishna-labi तिश्ना-लबी Having parched lips/ Thirst/Desire/Passion

Tohfatan तोहफ़तन As a gift

Tohfa-e-tar तोहफ़ा-ए-तर Welcome or prized gift

Tohmat तोहमत False accusation/Allegation

Tugyaanii तुग़यानी Flood/ Deluge/Inundation/ Overflowing/Storm/ Strong/Powerful/ Excess/Forceful/ Exorbitance (weather)

Tuhuur तुहूर Water of paradise

Tukhm तुख्म Seed/Sperm/ Egg/Progeny/Children/

Origin(Metaphorically)/ Offspring

Tuluu-e-mehr तुलु-ए-मैहर Sunrise

Tund तुंद Swift/Hot- tempered/Fierce/Acrid/ Pungent/Caustic

Tund-o-tez-rau तुंद-ओ- तेज़-रौ Quick and fast- paced

Tunuk तुनुक Slender/ Weak/Thin/Slight/ Delicate

Tunuk-zarfi तुनुक-ज़र्फ़ी Cheapness/Irritable nature/Shallow temperament

Tund-khuu तुण्ड-खू Furious/ Fretful/Passionate

Turaab तुराब Earch/Ground

Turaabii तुराबी Earthen/ Earthy

Turbat तुर्बत Tomb

Turfa तुफ़्रा Strange/ Agreeable/Novel/ Extraordinary/Rare/ Wonderful

Turra-e-dastaar तुर्रा-ए-दस्तार Adornment of turban

Tursh तुर्श Sour/Acid/Harsh/Ill-tempered

Tuubaa तूबा Tree with sweet fruit

Tuul तूल Length/Long/Effusiveness

Tuur तूर Mount/Hill/Mount Sinai

U

Khvaabon ke ufuq par tiraa chehra ho hamesha
Aur main usii chehre se nae khvaab sajaauun
Athar Nafees

Had chaahiye sazaa men uquubat ke vaaste
Aakhir gunahgaar huun kaafir nahiin huun main
Mirza Ghalib

Aanch aatii hai tire jism kii uryaanii se
Pairahan hai ki sulagtii huii shab hai koii
Nasir Kazmi

Zinda rahne ke the jitne usluub
Zindagii kat gaii tab yaad aae
Sadique Naseem

Sardii aur garmii ke uzr nahiin chalte
Mausam dekh ke saahab ishq nahiin hotaa
Moin Shadab

Dil kii dahliiz pe jab shaam kaa saaya utraa
Ufuq-e-dard se siine men ujaalaa utraa
Hasan Abidi

Mujh ko auron se kuchh nahiin hai kaam
Tujh se har dam umiid-vaarii hai
Faez Dehlvi

Dilon kii uqda-kushaaii kaa vaqt hai ki nahiin
Ye aadmii kii khudaaii kaa vaqt hai ki nahiin
Aziz Hamid Madni

Faaqon se tang aae to poshaak bech dii
Uryaan hue to shab kaa andheraa pahan liyaa
Bedil Haidri

Hai nagiina har ek uzv-e-badan
Tum ko kyaa ehtiyaaj zevar kii
Imdad Ali Bahr

U

Ubhaar उभार Rising/ Swelling/Aquiring fullness/Exitement/ Persuasion

Uftaada उफ़्तादा Fallen

Ufuq उफ़ुक़ Horizon/ Region of earth

Ufuq-e-dard उफ़ुक़-ए-दर्द Horizon or region of pain

Ujlat उज्लत Haste/Hurry

Ujlat-e-kaar उज्लत-ए-कार Hasty

Ujrat उज्रत Fee/Wages/ Remuneration/Apology

Umaaraa उमारा Rich

Umam उमम Peoples/ Nations/Tribes/Sects/ Followers

Ummaton उम्मतों Followers

Ummid-vaarii उम्मीद-वारी Candidacy/Candidature/ Expectancy

Umr-e-guzishta उम्र-ए-गुज़िश्ता Past life

Umr-e-raftaa उम्र-ए-रफ़्ता Past life/Past time/ Elapsed time

Umr-e-taabiiii उम्र-ए-ताबीई Natural age

Uns उन्स Attachment/ Affection/Friendship/ Love

Unsur उन्सुर Element/ Part/Component/Factor

Unvaan उन्वान Preface/ Introduction/Title/ Heading/Title of a book

Uqaabii उक़ाबी Hawkish/ Falcon-like

Uqda उक़्दा Knot/ Entanglement/Secret/ Mystery/Complicated affair/Knotty problem/ Confused state

Uqda-kusha उक़्दा -कुशा Problem solver/One who removes another's difficulties

Uqda-kushaaii उक़्दा-कुशाई Open knots/ Solving or removing a problem or difficulty

Uquubat उक़ूबत Punishment/ Chastisement/ Persecution

Uruuj उरूज Pinnacle/ Zenith/Height/ Elevation/Success/ Progress/Exaltation/ Climax/Ascension/ Rising

Uruuj-e-aadam-e-khakii उरूज-ए-आदम-ए-ख़ाकी Height attained by Adam's dust

Uruus उरूस Bride

Uruus-e-bahaar उरूस-ए-बहार Bride of spring

Uruus-e-nau उरूस-ए-नौ New bride

Uryaan उर्यां Naked

Uryaani उर्यानी Nakedness

Ushshaaq उश्शाक़ Lovers

Usluub उस्लूब Manner/ Method/Way/Style

Usthukhvaan उस्तुख़वां Skeleton

Ustuvaar उस्तुवार Firm/ Strong/Powerful/ Secure/Durable/Even/ Level/Equal

Uyuub उयूब Defects/Faults

Uzr उज़्र Regret/Denial/ Excuse/Pretext/ Apology/Plea

Uzv उज़्व Part

Uzv-e-badan उज़्व-ए-बदन Parts of the body

Uzv-e-tan उज़्व-ए-तन Part of body

V

Aankhon men terii dekh rahaa huun main apnii shakl
Ye koii vaahima ye koii khvaab to nahiin
Shahryar

Vaarafta huun aisaa men ki kuuche men butaan ke
Thahraauun jo tuk dil ko to phir paanv ukhad jaae
Mushafi Ghulam Hamdani

Taazgii hai sukhan-e-kuhna men ye baad-e-vafaat
Log aksar mire jiine kaa gumaan rakhte hain
Imam Bakhsh Nasikh

Ye vaqfa saaaton kaa chand sadiyon ke baraabar hai
Vo ab aavaaz dete hain to pahchaanii nahiin jaatii
Khalid Hasan Qadiri

'Kaif' paidaa kar samundar kii tarah
Vusaten khaamoshiyaan gahraaiyaan
Kaif Bhopali

Mittii kii mohabbat men ham aashufta-saron ne
Vo qarz utaare hain ki vaajib bhii nahiin the
Iftikhar Arif

Vabaa ne kaash hamen bhii bulaa liyaa hotaa
To ham pe maut kaa ehsaan bhii nahiin hotaa
Rahat Indori

Bade vasuuq se duniyaa fareb detii rahii
Bade khuluus se ham etibaar karte rahe
Shaukat Wasti

Mohabbaten na rahiin us ke dil men mere liye
Magar vo miltaa thaa hans kar ki vaza-daar jo thaa
Rajinder Manchanda Bani

Tire badalne ke baa-vasf tujh ko chaahaa hai
Ye etiraaf bhii shaamil mire gunaah men hai
Parveen Shakir

V

Vaa वा To open or tell/ Expose/Denoting diminution or contempt/ Open/Again/Expression of pain/Re-

Vaabasta वाबस्ता Bound together/ Related/Connected/ Dependent/Subservient

Vabastagii वाबस्तगी Affinity

Vaada-e-sabr-e-aazmaa वादा-ए-सब्र-ए-आज़मा Patience-testing promise

Vaadi वादी Valley/Vale/ Passage/Route/Forest/ Desert/Obstinacy

Vaahid वाहिद One/ Unique/Singular/Sole/ One (attributive name of God)

Vaahima वाहिमा Whim/ Hallucination/Fancy/ Imagination

Vaajib वाजिब Appropriate/ Just/Right/Expedient/ Proper/Necessary/ Incumbent/Obligatory / Reasonable

Vaalaa-nizhaadon वाला-निज़्हादों Born of superior rulers

Vaamaanda वामांदा Tired

Vaaraftaa वारफ़्ता Infatuated/Distracted/ Mad/Lost/Gone astray

Vaarastagii वारस्तगी Deliverance

Vaare वारे Offered/
Benefits/Gains

Vaashud वाशुद Opened

Vaashud-e-gul वाशुद-ए-
गुल Open flower

Vaazeh वाज़ेह Evident

Vaazhguunii वाज़हगूनी
Being inverted

Vabaa वबा Epidemic/
Pandemic/Pestilence/
Plague/Social evil/Social
malpractice/Contagion

Vabaal वबाल Calamity/
Burden/Load/Curse/
Misfortune/Plague/
Pestilence

Vabaal-e-dosh वबाल-ए-
दोश Heavy burden on
shoulder/Painful/Cause
of trouble

Vadiiat वदीअत Reward

Vafaa वफ़ा Loyalty/
Faithfulness/
Fulfillment/Fulfilling a
promise/Keeping one's
promise

Vafaa-shiaar वफ़ा-शिआर
Faithful/Loyal/Sincere

Vafaat वफ़ात Death/
Demise

Vafuur वफ़ूर Excess

Vahdat वहदत Unity

Vahii वही Divine revelation

Vahiid वहीद Unique/
Unrivalled/
Incomparable/
Singular/Individual/A
characteristic name of
God

Vahshat-zadaa वहशत-
ज़दा Bewildered/Awe-
struck/Aghast

Vahshii वहशी Wild/
Savage/Barbaric/
Uncivilised/Crazy/
Untamed/Brute

Vale वले Yet/But/However

Valek वलेक But

Vaja वजा Pain/Ache/
Disease/Affliction/
Complaint/Mourning

Vajab वजब Maximum
distance between thumb
and little finger, around
9 inches

Vajd वज्द Ecstasy/ Rapture/Excessive love/Religious or poetic frenzy/Overwhelming emotions

Vajuud वजूद Existence/ Being/Substance/Life

Vajuud-e-zan वजूद-ए-ज़न Existence of woman

Vaqaar वक़ार Honour/ Reputation/Dignity/ Reputation

Vaqaar-e-dast-e-dua वक़ार-ए-दस्त-ए-दुआ Dignity of the praying hand

Vaqaar-e-khun-e-shahidaan-e-karbala वक़ार-ए-ख़ून-ए-शहीदां-ए-कर्बला Honour of blood of martyrs of Karbala

Vaqf वक़्फ़ Devoting (one's life)/Stopping/Standing/ Permanence/Constancy/ Trust/Endowment/ Understanding/ Intelligence

Vaqfa वक़्फ़ा Interval/ Interlude/Intermission/ Delay/Hiatus/Respite

Vaqf-e-khalish वक़्फ़-ए-ख़लिश Engaged in pricking

Vaqt-e-giriya वक़्त-ए-गिरिया Time of mourning

Vasf वस्फ़ Attribute/ Quality/Merit/Virtue/ Character/Description/ Expression of qualities

Vasiia वसीअ Large/ Ample/Capacious/ Spacious/Roomy/Wide

Vasiile वसीले Means/ Supports/Mediations/ Intercessions

Vasuuq वसूक़ Confidence/ Trust/Reliance/ Dependence/Strength/ Steadfastness/Firmness

Vasvase वस्वसे Whims

Vatiira वतीरा Disposition/ Mannerism/Behaviour/ Habit/Way

Vazaa वज़ा Condition/
State/Conduct/
Behaviour/Manner/Style

Vaza-daar वज़ा-दार
Dignified/Elegant/
Stylish

Vaza-daarii
वज़ा-दारी Courtesy/
Manners

Vazaahat वज़ाहत
Explanation/
Vivid description/
Clarification/Refinement

Vazf वस्फ़ Praise/Merit/
Virtue/Narrative/
Expression of qualities/
Attribute/Trait/
Character/Description/
Prescribing/Quality

Vilaadat विलादत Birth

Vusat वुसअत Expanse

Vusat-e-daaman-e-dil
वुसअत-ए-दामन-ए-दिल
Vastness of hem of the
heart

Vusaten वुसअतें
Dimensions/Space/
Area/Latitude/
Amplitude

Fazaa-e-dil pe kahiin chhaa na jaae yaas kaa rang
Kahaan ho tum ki badalne lagaa hai ghaas kaa rang
Ahmad Mushtaq

Jitne bikhre hue kaagaz hain vo yakjaa kar le
Raat chupke se kahaa aa ke havaa ne ham se
Munawwar Rana

Javaab dhuund ke saare jahaan se jab laute
Hamen to kar gayaa yaklakht laa-javaab koii
Khaleel Mamoon

Ham ishq men hain fard to tum husn men yaktaa
Ham saa bhii nahiin ek jo tum saa nahiin koii
Lala Madhav Ram Jauhar

Aur hii vo log hain jin ko hai yazdaan kii talaash
Mujh ko insaanon kii duniyaa men hai insaan kii talaash
Nazeer Siddiqui

Ab na vo shorish-e-raftaar na vo josh-e-junuun
Ham kahaan phans gae yaaraan-e-subuk-gaam ke saath
Ali Jawwad Zaidi

Is qadar naaz hai kyuun aap ko yaktaaii kaa
Duusraa naam hai vo bhii mirii tanhaaii kaa
Dagh Dehlvi

Yakum january hai nayaa saal hai
December men puuchhuungaa kyaa haal hai
Ameer Qazalbash

Hamaaraa zinda rahnaa aur marnaa ek jaisaa hai
Ham apne yaum-e-paidaaish ko bhii barsii samajhte hain
Farhat Ehsas

Yahiin husain bhii guzre yahiin yaziid bhii thaa
Hazaar rang men duubii huii zamiin huun main
Rahat Indori

Y

Yaad-dahaanii याद-दहानी Reminder

Yaaft याफ़्त Accessibility/ Availability/Bribe/ Earning/Income/Gain/ Profit/Perquisite

Yaara यारा Strength/ Courage/Power

Yaaraan-subuk-gaam यारां-सुबुक-गाम Fast-paced friends

Yaas यास Despair/ Hopelessness

Yagaana यगाना Unique/ Singular/Sole/ Unrivalled/One/Single/ Relation/True friend/ Kinsman

Yakbaar यक्बार Once

Yakjaaii यकजाई Union/ Unite/Join/Friendship/ Closeness

Yak-jehtii यक-जेहती Solidarity/Unity/ Unanimity/Singleness of purpose

Yak-jehtii-e-hayaat यक-जेहती-ए-हयात Unity of life

Yak-lahza यक-लहज़ा Once moment

Yaklakht यकलख़्त All at once/Suddenly

Yaksaan यकसां Same/ Equal/Alike/The same/ Even/Level/Collected/ Same all over

Yaksar यकसर All at once/ All together/Entire/ Totally/Completely/ Singing in the same tune

Yaktaa यक्ता Matchless

Yaktaaii यकताई Being unique or unequalled/ Unite/Agree

Yakum यकुम First/One/ First day of the month

Yaqiin-e-kaamil यक़ीन-ए-कामिल Utmost confidence

Yargalaam यर्गलाम Hostage

Yaum-e-paidaaish यौम-ए-पैदाइश Birthday

Yazdaan यज़दां God

Yaziid यज़ीद Cruelor tyrant ruler or person/Wicked/ Cursed/Execrable/The ruler in who reign Imam Hussain was martyred at Karbala

Z

Maanaa ki tuu zahiin bhii hai khuub-ruu bhii hai
Tujh saa na main huaa to bhalaa kyaa buraa huaa
Mohammad Alvi

Zar kaa banda ho ki mahruumii kaa maaraa huaa shakhs
Jis ko dekho vahii auqaat se niklaa huaa hai
Tauqeer Taqi

Ediyaan maar ke zakhmii bhii hue log magar
Koii chashma nahiin zarkhez zamiin se niklaa
Azlan Shah

Chale the yaar bade zoam men havaa kii tarah
Palat ke dekhaa to baithe hain naqsh-e-paa kii tarah
Ahmad Faraz

Mauquuf jurm hii pe karam kaa zuhuur thaa
Bande agar qusuur na karte qusuur thaa
Ameer Minai

Ye baat baat pe qaanuun-o-zaabte kii giraft
Ye zillaten ye gulaamii ye daur-e-majbuurii
Sahir Ludhianvi

Zindagii har zaaviye se dekhtaa huun main tujhe
Hai mirii fikr-o-nazar kaa daaera phailaa huaa
Jahangeer Nayab

Dil kii qiimat to mohabbat ke sivaa kuchh bhii na thii
Jo mile suurat-e-zebaa ke khariidaar mile
Jameel Malik

Kitne mah-o-anjum hain ziyaa-paash azal se
Lekin na huii kam dil-e-insaan kii siyaahii
Qadir Siddiqi

Kii mire qatl ke baad us ne jafaa se tauba
Haae us zuud-pashemaan kaa pashemaan honaa
Mirza Ghalib

Z

Zaabte ज़ाब्ते Rules and regulations

Zaad-e-safar ज़ाद-ए-सफ़र Provisions for the journey

Zaahid ज़ाहिद Hermit/ Ascetic/Recluse/ Devotee/Monk

Zaanuu ज़ानू Part between waist and knees while sitting on the knees

Zaar ज़ार Afflicted/ Lamenting/Fertile land/ Humble

Zaarii ज़ारी Crying/ Wailing/Lamenting/ Groaning/Supplication/ Entreaty/Plight/ Predicament

Zaat ज़ात Tribe/Caste/ Breed/Origin/Essence/ Sort/Kind/Substance/ Nature

Zaat-e-baht ज़ात-ए-बहृत The God/Holy/Pure being

Zaaviye ज़ाविए Angles

Zabh ज़बृह Slaughter/ Sacrifice

Zabiiha ज़बीहा Animal slaughteredand fit for food as per Islaic tenets/ Sacrificed

Zabuun ज़बूं Impure

Zad ज़द Target/Blow/ Range/Loss/Stroke/ Object of an aim/ Damage/Attack/Hit

Zada ज़दा Victim

Zadan ज़दन Infatuated

Zahe ज़हे Excellent

Zahid ज़हिद Devotee

Zahiin ज़हीं Intelligent/
Ingenious

Zahmat ज़हमत Trouble

Zahuur ज़हूर Manifestation

Zaiifon ज़ैफों Weak

Zaiff-o-zaar ज़ैफ-ओ-ज़ार
Weak and distressed

Zakaat ज़कात Charity

Zakhiira ज़ख़ीरा Treasure/
Hoard/Provision/
Victual

Zaliil-o-khvaar ज़लील-
ओ-ख्वार Insulted and
humiliated

Zamaam ज़माम Reins

Zamaam-e-kaar ज़माम-ए-
कार Control of
work

Zamaan ज़मां Time

Zamaana-e-haazir ज़माना-
ए-हाज़िर Present time/
Present tense

Zamaan-o-makaan ज़मान-
ओ-मकान Time and
place

Zamaana-saaz ज़माना-
साज़ Opportunist/
One who changes his
principles according to
the situation/Cunning

Zamiin-nazhaad Born of
earth

Zamzam ज़म-ज़म Well in
Kaba whose water is
considered holy/water
from this well

Zamzama-sanj ज़मज़मा-
संज Singer/One who
sings in a melodious
voice/Musician/Eulogist

Zamzama-sanjii ज़मज़मा-
संजी Music playing/
Sound like water falling

Zan ज़न Female

Zana ज़ना Bastardy/Lewd/
Infidelity

Zanaan ज़नान Women

Zanjiir-zanii ज़ंजीर-ज़नी
Chain

Zanakhdaan जनख़दां Dimple/Pit in chin

Zan-muriidii ज़न-मुरीदी Hen-pecked

Zar ज़र Gold

Zarar ज़रर Ruin/Damage/ Harm/Injury/Detriment

Zarb ज़र्ब Blow/Striking/ Multiplication/Beating/ Impression/Loss/ Damage/Stamping of coins

Zard ज़र्द Pale/Yellow/Dull

Zarf ज़र्फ़ Capability/Vase

Zarfii ज़र्फ़ी Shallowness

Zar-fishaaniyaan ज़र-फ़िशानिआं Gold sprinkling

Zariif ज़रीफ़ Humorous/ Witty/Jocular/Jovial/ Comical/Clever/ Ingenious/Smart/ Handsome

Zarkhez ज़रखेज़ Fertile/ Rich soil/Productive

Zau ज़ौ Glow/Light

Zauq ज़ौक़ Derive pleasure from/ Taste/Appreciation/ Enjoyment/Talent/ Verve/Relish

Zauq-e-nazar ज़ौक़-ए-नज़र Perceptive eye/ Connoisseur

Zauq-e-tamaasha ज़ौक़-ए-तमाशा Appreciation of spectacle

Zauq-e-yaqiin ज़ौक़-ए-यक़ीन Gift of belief

Zavaal ज़वाल Afternoon when the sun is on the decline/Decline/Decay/ Failure/Cessation

Zeb ज़ेब Beauty/Elegance/ Grace/Adornment/ Adorning/Imparting grace to/Decorating

Zebaa ज़ेबा Adorned/ Beautiful

Ze-bas ज़े-बस In abundance/Sufficiently/ Plentifully

Zeb-e-gullu ज़ेब-ए-गुल्लू
Adornment of the neck

Zee-e-daam ज़ी-ए-दाम
Trap/Defeat

Ze-haal-e-miskiin ज़े-हाल-ए-मिस्कीन Plight of the poor

Zer ज़ेर Under

Zera-zera ज़ेरा-ज़ेरा Piece/Scrap/Bit/Atom/Desire

Zer-e-lab ज़ेर-ए-लब
Quietly/In whispers/in an undertone

Zer-o-zabar ज़ेर-ओ-ज़बर
Topsy-turvy/Turned upside down/To ransack/To disintegrate/Over-turned/Ruined

Zi-bas ज़ि-बस Only

Zi-bas-ki ज़ि-बस-कि The side of/On the part of/Much as

Zihaanat ज़िहानत
Intelligence

Ziinat ज़ीनत Grace

Ziin-saazii ज़ीन-साज़ी
Saddling up

Zikr-e-huur ज़िक्र-ए-हूर
Description of Houris, the beautiful woman promised to the devout in Heaven

Zillaten ज़िल्लतें
Insult/Dishonour/Disgrace

Zindaan ज़िंदां Prison

Zinhaar ज़िन्हार Care, Protection

Ziyaa ज़िया Light/Splendour/Blaze

Ziyaad ज़ियाद Increase/Augment

Ziyaan ज़ियां Loss/Damage/Injury/Hurt/Detriment

Ziyaa-paash ज़िया-पाश
Light breaking

Ziyaarat ज़ियारत Visiting a shrine/Pilgrimage/Seeing or visiting a holy place/Shrine or a holy person

Ziyaarat-gaah ज़ियारत-गाह Place of pilgrimage

Zoaf ज़ोअफ़ Weak/Feeble

Zoam ज़ोअम Pride/Conceit

Zof ज़ोफ़ Weakness/ Feebleness/Debility/ Infirmity/Imbecility of mind or body

Zof-e-basaarat ज़ोफ़-ए-बसारत Weakness of eyesight

Zohad ज़ोहद Religious devotion

Zohra ज़ोहरा Bright/ Beauteous/Planet Venus

Zohra-jabiinon ज़ोहरा-जबीनों Venus-faced (plural)

Zor ज़ोर Force/Strength/ Power/Influence

Zubuun जुबूं Wicked/Evil/ Unlucky/Faulty

Zuhuur जुहूर Appearing/ Becoming visible/ Manifestation/Visibility/ Coming to pass/The act of appearance/Advent/ Coming of Imam Mehdi

Zuhuur-e-tartiib जुहूर-ए-तरतीब Meticulously arranged

Zulf-e-dotaa जुल्फ़-ए-दोता Braided hair

Zulmat जुल्मत Darkness/ Dark place/Region of darkness/Ignorance

Zuud जूद Quick/Swift/ Quickly/Suddenly/Soon